"F
ositi
not t!
who
The'
Thor
ly u
unde
New
son
and
thro'
the
of
tent
stres
faith
himse
"othe
    Th
have
tional S

cent decades, and m... ... ... working in the tradition of Joseph Maréchal and Karl Rahner. PERSONAL FAITH represents a further development of their pioneering work on integration in a comprehensive synthesis of Scholasticism and Phenomenology. Carlos Cirne-Lima conceives faith as personal knowledge, as the cognitive moment of one's free commitment to the divine person who is Christ. In this act of freely determined, concrete knowledge those deeper dimensions of Christ's person which are disclosed become the basis for a more and more trusting surrender to him.

PERSONAL FAITH has been described by *The Modern Schoolman* as one of the major works of this past decade; and Gerald McCool, S.J., writing in *Thought,* has praised it as, "one of the most ambitious attempts yet undertaken to harmonize the results of a phenomenology of human knowledge with the dynamic metaphysics of the incarnate spirit." In his Foreword, Professor James Collins commends Carlos Cirne-Lima for his "admirable balance of mind in making both a phenomenological and metaphysical study of faith": "Cirne-Lima invites us . . . to see for ourselves that the virtue of divine faith does not remain aloof from men but makes itself at home in their own ever recognizable human reality." PERSONAL FAITH will be acknowledged by all Catholic theologians and philosophers as a challenging and stimulating contribution to the rethinking of traditional Thomism which pontiffs from Leo XIII onward have called for.

PERSONAL FAITH

PERSONAL FAITH

A Metaphysical Inquiry

CARLOS CIRNE-LIMA

Translated by
G. Richard Dimler, S.J.

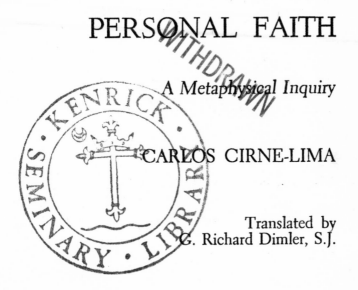

HERDER AND HERDER

1965
HERDER AND HERDER NEW YORK
232 Madison Avenue, New York 10016

Original edition: *Der Personale Glaube.*
Eine erkenntnismetaphysische Studie,
Verlag Felizian Rauch, Innsbruck, 1959.

Imprimi potest: John M. Daley, S.J.
Provincial, Baltimore Province

Nihil obstat: Patrick A. Barry
Censor Librorum

Imprimatur: Patrick C. Brennan
Vicar General, Diocese of Burlington
October 7, 1964
The nihil obstat and imprimatur are official declarations that a book
or pamphlet is free of doctrinal or moral error. No implication is contained therein that those who have granted the nihil obstat or imprimatur agree with the contents, opinions or statements expressed.

Library of Congress Catalog Card Number: 64–19726
© 1965 by Herder and Herder, Incorporated
Printed in the United States of America

Contents

From the inception of the modern world, philosophers and theologians have kept the question of faith in a constant ferment. A good deal of energy has gone into the directly apologetic and counterapologetic activities of defending and attacking the content of various faith propositions. This wearing approach has led to a series of stalemates between the controversialists representing different confessions or else, as in the case of the Enlightenment view of natural religion, to a complete evisceration of the problem of faith. In the light of such frustrating experiences, thoughtful men have been prompted to look critically at the assumption that the question of faith must be treated mainly in terms of the propositional content of faith. The lesson of the whole modern discussion is that this content, while an indispensable component in the faith situation, cannot be respected and adequately studied apart from the act of faith.

Here, as well as on so many other issues of urgency for present-day believers, the turning point came in 1870 with the publication of Cardinal Newman's *A Grammar of Assent*. Newman strongly defended the intellectual aspect of the content of faith, the need to subject it to cool analysis, and the importance of expressing one's findings in propositional form. But with equal firmness he pointed out that the affirmed content of religious faith is indissolubly bound up with the act of believing, and that it is the task and glory of the modern mind to bring the latter into full relief and thus recover the integral context for every propositional statement of faith. Whatever the details of his position, Newman took seriously the personal character of faith and every religious relationship founded on the act of faith. He underlined, in a manner that could never be forgotten thereafter, the opening up of person to person as being the essential achievement of the faith act. The content which the believer affirms would lose its proper significance as religious truth were it not seen by him to be entailed by his personal response to the personal God.

Another significant step in reawakening the problem of faith was taken by Max Scheler and the phenomenologists of religion who followed in his wake. Their aim was to develop in depth the description of the religious attitude, with special emphasis upon the way in which faith displays itself in one's personal existence and in the interpersonal community of men. Instead of keeping the faith attitude at a distance, as had been dictated by the controversialists' type of procedure, these thinkers guided their analyses by the actual human relationships presented by living believers. They found that the faith act has an internal structure distinctively its own, and that its leading characteristic is to lead beyond the believer himself to the personal reality of the other. In this respect, religious faith in God is not utterly unlike the ordinary good faith which holds among human persons. The existential personalist philoso-

phers, notably Karl Jaspers and Gabriel Marcel, worked
upon this clue in order to bring out a common human
structure of faith, in respect to which the workings of religious faith can be better understood and its basis of
certitude more carefully weighed. Not only intentional
description but also a verification of personally ascertained
evidence became a task for the philosopher of religion and
the theologian who grasped the bearing of philosophical
work upon his own field.

More recently, the question has been raised whether any
positive relationship can be established between these contemporary analyses of the faith situation and the vast body
of scholastic thought. What makes this issue acute is the
fact that an alliance made exclusively between the phenomenology of faith and the views of man-the-believer contained in Scripture and the fathers has not proven to be
fully satisfactory. For it still leaves the certitude and truth-
claim of divine faith exposed to technical philosophical
criticism, which is not met on its own level by a restrictive
union between patristic and phenomenological forms of
personalism. It can no longer simply be assumed that the
long intellectual tradition of men of faith laboring in the
scholastic modes of thought is irrelevant for the personalist
conception of the act and content of faith, or is incompatible with it. All the human efforts at understanding the
mystery of faith and relating it to our other modes of being
and knowing must be drawn together. Intellectual coopera-
tion on this central matter cannot acknowledge any restrictive covenants, which would deprive us of the cumula-
tive labors of many reflective minds.

On the historical side, a good start has been made by

Josef Pieper in his investigations into the Thomistic notion of faith. He has brought out that St. Thomas himself is most careful to join the analysis of the content of faith with that of the act of faith, and to integrate both aspects under the decisive theme of the personal relationship freely established between the human believer and the revealing God. In addition, attempts are now under way to make an original speculative reformulation of the basic Thomistic principles, insofar as they bear upon the human existent and his dynamic relationships of knowing and willing. Encouraged by the pioneer research done by Joseph Maréchal and challenged by Martin Heidegger's rethinking of the entire question of being, a group of German-speaking Jesuit philosophers and theologians has started to re-do the theory of knowledge and metaphysics, anthropology and ethics, in a way that makes the intellectual resources of past centuries of reflection operative within the context of our age. This movement centers around Rahner and Lotz, Coreth and Brunner, all of whom feel the need for enriching the present discussion of the nature of religious faith with the fruitful thoughts drawn from the medieval and modern schoolmen.

The present book by Carlos Cirne-Lima reflects all of these modern tendencies, especially that of the last-named group. Its special task and value consist in showing how some far-flung philosophical theories can be brought to bear, with sharp clarity and orderliness, upon the problem of faith. One need not agree with the author's views on intuition and the intelligible species in order to appreciate his accomplishment of presenting some familiar views in a new light, designed to illuminate the perpetually troubling topics of the object, truth and certitude of faith. He displays admirable balance of mind in making both a phenomenological and a metaphysical study of faith and its relations with other modes of knowing. And he shows the undeniable need for having an adequate epistemology, if one seeks to achieve any philosophical rigor in the phenomenological description or metaphysical analysis of man's religious faith. A synthesis of all these factors is reached in the culminating theory of personal knowledge, which sinks its roots into the human instances of interpersonal relationship and then uses this analogy to interpret the communion between the man of religious faith and God.

Perhaps the strongest impression left by this book is that its author respects the complex reality of faith. His fundamental refusal to oversimplify the difficulties is reflected in several admirable features: the use of more than one method of analysis, the view of faith as a personal act nourished by a real content, the dialectic established between the believer's reception of the personal reality of God and his active acceptance of the statements and commands made by the God-man, and the careful balance between the cognitive and volitional elements in the free decision of personal faith. Cirne-Lima invites us in turn to wrestle with these difficulties, and thus to see for ourselves that the virtue of divine faith does not remain aloof from men but makes itself at home in their own ever recognizable human reality.

JAMES COLLINS

1 PROBLEM AT ISSUE AND METHODOLOGY

What is faith? What happens when I believe in a "Thou"? Is such knowledge personal? What is meant by personal? What role does the free will play in such knowledge? What is the origin of the certitude of faith? These are philosophical questions. We intend to treat them philosophically and answer them philosophically.

This series of questions can be numbered also among the classical problems of theology. The inquiry into the nature of faith entails an encounter not only with the great men of the middle ages, Thomas Aquinas, Bonaventure, Duns Scotus, but also with modern theologians like Laberthonnière,[1] Mallet,[2] Billot,[3] Gardeil,[4] Rousselot,[5] Karl

[1] L. Laberthonnière, *Essais de Philosophie Religieuse*, Paris 1903; *Le Réalisme Chrétien et l'Idéalisme Grec*, Paris 1904. Both works were placed on the Index in 1906.

[2] F. Mallet, "L'unité complexe du problème de la foi," *Revue du Clergé Français* 53, 1908, 257ff; "Un entretien avec M. Blondel," *RCF* 27, 1901, 627–636; "D'où naissent quelques malentendus persistants en apologétique?" *RCF* 32, 1902, 12–31; "Qu'est-ce que la foi?" Paris 1907, 2nd ed.

[3] L. Billot, *De Ecclesia*, vol. 1, Rome 1898; *De Virtutibus Infusis*, Rome 1901.

[4] A. Gardeil, "La crédibilité," *Revue Thomiste* 13, 1905, 5–28, 125–146, 278–295, 633–645; 14, 1906, 127–144, 511–528; 15, 1907, 18–35; *La Crédibilité et l'Apologétique*, Paris 1907.

Adam,[6] Mouroux,[7] Aubert,[8] August Brunner[9] and others
who have labored over the same problem. It requires a discussion of the question of the *analysis fidei*, an old problem,
it is true, yet one which remains modern, because it is still
unsolved; and it demands as well a new inquiry whose explicit theme is the personal element involved in the act of
faith. Cardinal Newman,[10] Mouroux and August Brunner
have devoted themselves particularly to the study of the
personal element in faith. And any study of it undertaken
today must also include a dialogue with modern Protestant
theologians such as Emil Brunner,[11] or Karl Barth.[12] Even

[5] P. Rousselot, *L'intellectualisme de St. Thomas*, Paris 1936, 3rd
ed.; "Les yeux de la foi," *Recherches de Science Religieuse* I, 1910,
241–259, 444–475; "Remarques sur l'histoire de la notion de foi
naturelle," *RSR* 4, 1913, 1–36.

[6] K. Adam, *Glaube und Glabenswissenschaft im Katholizismus*
(Rottenburg, 1923) 2 ed.; *The Spirit of Catholicism*, tr. Dom
Justin McCann O.S.B., New York 1930; *The Son of God*, tr. Philip
Hereford, New York 1957; *Christ Our Brother*, tr. Dom Justin
McCann O.S.B., New York 1939.

[7] J. Mouroux, *I Believe. The Personal Structure of Faith*, tr.
Michael Turner, New York 1959.

[8] R. Aubert, *Le problème de l'acte de foi. Donnés traditionnelles
et résultats des controverses récents*, Louvain 1950, 2nd ed.

[9] A. Brunner, *Glaube und Erkenntnis. Philosophisch-theologische
Darlegung*, Munich 1951.

[10] J. H. Newman, *A Grammar of Assent*, New York 1955; see J.
Boekraad, *The Personal Conquest of Truth According to J. H.
Newman*, Louvain 1955.

[11] E. Brunner, *Offenbarung und Vernunft. Die Lehre von der
christlichen Glaubenserkenntnis*, Zurich 1941; *Das Symbolische in
der religiösen Erkenntnis. Beiträge zu einer Theorie des religiösen
Erkennens*, Tübingen 1914; *Philosophie und Offenbarung*, Tübingen 1925; *Religionsphilosophie, protestantische Theologie*, Munich
1927.

aside from the discussion proper to the act of faith itself, the problem of the nature of personal faith arises very frequently in theology today. Is not baptism a sacramental incarnation of faith, to be understood in terms of faith itself? Can we speak of the sacrament of penance without conceiving of repentance as faith risen again to life? Is not every sacrament in the last analysis faith which has become visible in the context of the Church? Is not the Church herself "communal faith" in its historical dimensions?

To inquire into personal faith then is not to confine ourselves to a specifically Christian context. It is to set out on the same road Max Scheler,[13] Karl Jaspers[14] and Le Roy[15] have traveled. For faith has become a problem even for the philosopher.

From this broad and much-discussed complexus of questions we shall select out a single aspect. Our inquiry concerns the metaphysical structure of interpersonal faith. Its aim will be a metaphysical understanding of the faith which comes into being as the bond between one man and another.

---

[12] K. Barth, Kirchliche Dogmatik, vol. 1, Zollikon 1939, 3rd ed., 239–260; Church Dogmatics, vol. 1, Edinburgh 1936; Anselm's Proof of the Existence of God in the Context of His Theological Scheme, Richmond, Va. 1960. See H. U. von Balthasar, Karl Barth. Darstellung und Deutung seiner Theologie, Cologne 1951, 148–168.

[13] M. Scheler, On the Eternal in Man, tr. Bernard Noble, London 1960.

[14] K. Jaspers, Psychologie der Weltanschauungen, Berlin 1954, 4th ed.; Der Philosophische Glaube, Munich 1955, 4th ed.; The Perennial Scope of Philosophy, tr. Ralph Manherin, New York 1949.

[15] E. Le Roy, Introduction à l'étude du problème religieux, Paris 1944; Dogme et critique, Paris 1907.

Metaphysics has been defined by Aristotle as the knowledge of being as being. Not the concrete determination of this existent or that, but that through which being is being is the subject of its consideration. This inquiry into the being of an existent supersedes all other questions insofar as metaphysics, inquiring into the ultimate foundation of the existent, seeks to comprehend the multiplicity of a limited essence in the light of its source. Accordingly, metaphysics is the science which must discover, through its own resources, the ground of its knowledge concerning each single being. It must therefore trace every individual back to its first beginning and bring to light its ultimate perfection. This metaphysics must do, since its task is to ground each determined existent in being itself. Metaphysics then is at once knowledge of the ultimate ground of being and knowledge of all beings.

In order to understand the existent in its being I must know what being is. And yet I know what being means, otherwise I could not be able to ask about it at all. For we cannot even ask about what is completely unknown to us.

My understanding of being, a knowledge of it which is at the same time a lack of knowledge of it, is an immediate insight which nonetheless must be philosophically explained and grounded. It is an immediacy, yet one which must be mediated through a reasoning process. For an intuition, legitimate though it may be, demands a scientific explanation of its possibility and its necessity.

By inquiring into the being of the existent I must necessarily inquire into my knowledge about being. Metaphysics is essentially a transcendental philosophy. Since it asks about everything, its inquiry is necessarily turned back upon itself, and so metaphysics becomes transcendental philosophy. I ask about the being of the existent and therefore ask about the being of the question also. Thus the question about being is seen to be the radical beginning which justifies itself because it involves itself in the questioning. This is metaphysics.

Thus it is clear that a special question becomes a metaphysical one only at the point of its insertion into the all-embracing question about being. Metaphysical discussion of any given object is possible therefore only within a system. For knowledge of the singular, in order to be metaphysical, must be comprehended and determined by knowledge of the whole. If we want to discuss any given object metaphysically then we must carry on this discussion within a system and on the basis of a system. If we do not do this, unexplained presuppositions, unanalyzed connections and unforeseen consequences are unavoidable.

To set down a complete system of philosophy however is a task which today more than ever is beyond the capacity of an individual thinker. Even the mere outline of a system seems scarcely within our power.

From what we have said, it is clear that there is only one way of dealing with our subject, without overstepping the narrow confines of this book. We will do justice to the concept of metaphysics only if we pose the special question concerning the nature of interpersonal belief in the general framework of the question about being, and only if we attempt to find our answer to it within this context. Our system however, that is to say, our universal theory of being and knowledge, can only be outlined in its essential structure. In this we see both the essential limits and also the

justification of the special question to which our inquiry
is directed.

These considerations also condition our method of treat-
ing the subject we have chosen to consider. After a brief
phenomenological description of interpersonal faith we
shall ask the all-encompassing question about being and
indicate the first elements of its metaphysical mediation.
From the question itself the "I" and the "Other" emerge.
Then the structure of sense-knowledge, of the cognitive
being-with-another and of the turning-back-upon-oneself
of knowledge in the process of abstraction can be outlined.
From this we shall attempt to derive intuition, that is, the
nonconceptual immediacy of human knowledge. This will
be treated extensively, since it is so important for an understanding of faith. Returning to the question of being we
shall attempt to show that the inquiry into being presupposes as its transcendental condition of possibility essentially personal knowledge. This personal knowledge, i.e.
faith, placed in another, a human "Thou," will then be discussed so that its fundamental structure may reveal itself.
Finally, the most important logical properties of faith will
be analyzed separately. In the appendix the completed
theory on the nature of belief will be applied to the
theological problem of faith, particularly to the question
of the analysis fidei.

In our general theory of being and knowledge, our view-
point is basically the same as that of J. Maréchal,[16] G.

[16] J. Maréchal, Le point de départ de la métaphysique. Leçons
sur le dévelopment historique et théorique du problème de la con-
naissance, Paris 1944–1947, vols. 1–5.

Siewerth,[17] K. Rahner,[18] J. B. Lotz,[19] W. Brugger[20] and E. Coreth,[21] to whom we owe an especial debt of gratitude.

[17] G. Siewerth, *Die Metaphysik der Erkenntnis nach Thomas von Aquin*, part I, *Die Sinnliche Erkenntnis*, Munich/Berlin 1933; *Der Thomismus als Identitätssystem*, Frankfurt am Main 1939; *Wort und Bild. Eine Ontologische Interpretation*, Düsseldorf 1952; *Thomas von Aquin. Die Menschliche Willensfreiheit*, Düsseldorf 1954; *Die Sinne und der Wert*, Düsseldorf 1956; *Metaphysik der Kindheit*, Einsiedeln 1957; *Der Mensch und sein Leib*, Einsiedeln 1953; *Die Apriorität der menschlichen Erkenntnis nach Thomas von Aquin: Symposion, Jahrbuch für Philosophie*, vol. 1, Freiburg i Br. 1949.

[18] K. Rahner, *Geist in Welt. Zur Metaphysik der endlichen Erkenntnis bei Thomas von Aquin*, Munich 1957, 2nd ed.; *Hörer des Wortes. Zur Grundlegung einer Religionsphilosophie*, Munich 1942. See also *Schriften zur Theologie*, Einsiedeln 1954–1956, vols. 1–3. *Theological Investigations*, vol. 1, tr. Cornelius Ernst O.P., Baltimore 1961; vol. 2, tr. Karl-H. Kruger, Baltimore 1963.

[19] J. B. Lotz, *Das Urteil und das Sein. Eine Grundlegung der Metaphysik*, Munich 1957.

[20] W. Brugger, *Das Unbedingte in Kants 'Kritik der reinen Vernunft': Kant und die Scholastik heute*, ed. J. B. Lotz, 1955, 109–153.

[21] E. Coreth, *Metaphysik als Aufgabe. Aufgaben der Philosophie. Drei Versuche von E. Coreth S.J., O. Muck S.J., J. Schasching S.J.;* ed. E. Coreth S.J., Innsbruck 1958, 13–95

2   TOWARD A PHENOMENOLOGY
OF INTERPERSONAL FAITH

1   Faith and Probability

The expressions "belief" and "to believe" are used in very different significations. Very often a mere probability is intended. Thus for example, if people say: "I believe that it will be a fine day tomorrow." The expression "to believe" means here that this statement is not sufficiently substantiated, that we can therefore attribute to it no real certainty but only probability. But we speak of belief not only in regard to natural events but also in regard to unsubstantiated and merely probable assertions about a person, as, for example, in the sentence: "I believe he will not hold his position very long." We even use the expression "believe" in the sense of a greater or less probability when speaking about whole nations and historical events: "I do not believe that there will be war because of it." In all of these examples we are dealing with the same thing: a probable assertion, an assertion which cannot be taken too seriously because it possesses no real certainty, and which, as the speaker indicates, is an expression of his own subjective feeling rather than of the objective situation.

The same word can signify however a personal encounter

between two men, a commitment to a human Thou in whom we place complete trust. If I say to a person: "I believe you," this means that I let this person act for me cognitively. I see a situation not with my own eyes but with the eyes of this other person. I see this situation because this man is aware of it, insofar as he is aware of it, and to the extent that he communicates his knowledge of it to me. This commission granted to another[22] to be, as it were, my representative, in placing an act of knowledge—a frequent occurrence in everyday life—is only one instance of interpersonal relationship and, consequently, may not be detached from this personal context. We may not treat it simply as a pure act of the understanding. In certain things a machine could take the place of our own thought, as a computer does at times. But this substitution is not faith; we do not believe in a computer; we cannot place any genuine faith in it. Personal belief lies on another plane, and should not be confused with this sort of mechanical substitution. For we experience faith as an act of our whole person; not just of our understanding but of our will and of our feelings. Our making another our "cognitive representative," if it is to be called faith, must be coupled with a kind of personal commitment to him. This act of our personal center is faith in the proper sense.

Our age, which remains to some extent a rationalistic one and which still thinks in scientific categories, is inclined to reduce the second meaning of the word "faith" to the first. This means that personal belief is called belief only because it yields no certitude in interpersonal relationships but

[22] A. Brugger, *Glaube und Erkenntnis*, 50–70.

merely probability. Faith, it is said, is our acceptance of an uncertain proposition, even though it involves a faith which can be characterized as a personal commitment. Such is not the case. For this reduction of any and all belief to our acceptance of a proposition as merely probable does not do justice to the phenomena. For there is, most certainly, a personal faith which involves the highest possible certitude. Personal faith is sometimes an unconditional commitment to a Thou, to whom we give our total confidence. And in this faith we feel secure and safe. The certitude of this faith is so great that we can say: "I believe you, no matter what the whole world may say." A person gives himself totally to another and defies the world, as it were, to make an assertion opposed to his belief. And even if it should do so, he would stand firm in his faith. If there is then a personal faith which gives such certainty, we cannot maintain that "faith" means only probable knowledge. For if faith would imply in every case an assent given to merely probable assertions, there could be no certainty in faith at all.

It is self-evident that not every act of personal faith possesses such certainty. There is also a faith which is less certain. But every act of personal faith can possess some degree of certitude. And if every act of personal faith involves some degree of certainty, then personal faith cannot be reduced to a merely probable assent. For such an assent is "merely probable" and is not essentially personal. If then it is not that, we can scarcely say that personal belief is fundamentally nothing more than our acceptance of a proposition as merely probable. Such a reduction fails to do justice to the phenomena.

An objection might be raised at this point, namely that the certainty of this faith is merely a subjective feeling, and that objectively faith possesses no such certainty. To this it can be said that we are proceeding here at first according to a purely phenomenological method, and that, therefore, we are considering the "purely subjective side." Whether acceptance of a proposition as probable or whether a personal act of faith is objectively correct, or whether they involve objective certainty does not concern us at the moment. Nonetheless, subjectively, and therefore phenomenologically, each is essentially distinct from the other. One act is indeed experienced as always "merely probable." On the other hand, the other act, the personal act of faith, on occasion is experienced as highly certain, and it is always experienced as essentially personal. Thus we are led to the following conclusion. We cannot place the personal act of belief in the same category as the "mere acceptance of a proposition as probable," if we wish to do justice to the phenomena.

The expression "a belief" can have a twofold meaning: one is a proposition which is not well-grounded and is therefore taken as merely probable; the other is an act of knowledge which on occasion yields the highest certainty and is always essentially personal. Which of these two meanings is, philosophically speaking, the original one is not the concern of our inquiry. August Brunner shows that the second meaning is phenomenologically the primary one and indicates the analogy through which the derived meaning has arisen.[23] We need not delay further over this. It will be

---

[23] A. Brugger, *Glaube und Erkenntnis*, 82–128.

enough to maintain that faith in the proper sense of the word is a personal act, our making another our "cognitive representative," an act which is not to be identified with "taking a proposition as merely probable." This personal faith alone is what concerns us here.

2 Faith and Pseudo-Faith

If we turn our attention to the act of faith itself, we shall see that the act of faith cannot be considered simply a logical conclusion derived from a prior knowledge. It is not a logical conclusion derived from its premises in accordance with determined laws of logic. There is, to be sure, something of the sort, a process which is called in scholastic technical terminology *scientia testimonialis*.

Scientia testimonialis is had when, by means of a reasoning process, we come to the knowledge that a man's assertion in a given case should be accepted as true. If, for example, a bank employee goes to the manager of his bank and confesses that he has embezzled a certain amount of money, the manager will "believe" him. He will make further inquiries. The results of his investigation will confirm his "belief." The employee has really embezzled such and such an amount of money. On most occasions of this sort, however, we are not dealing with "faith" but with *scientia testimonialis*. From the amount of his confession, the manager "knew" that the statement of the employee was true. He knew that this employee was of sound mind; and that a mentally sound man does not confess an embezzlement if he did not really perpetrate it. Perhaps he also knew that the employee was in financial straits, and that therefore the embezzlement was all the more probable. Once he hears the confession, then, he "knows" that the assertion of his employee is true. Nevertheless this knowledge is not of a personal nature. It is the logical conclusion flowing from many more or less certain premises. These premises however are not absolutely certain. The employee could be protecting someone else. This is extremely unlikely but it is still possible. And the conclusion, the knowledge of the embezzlement, the "belief" (i.e. *scientia testimonialis*) has only as much certitude as the premises possess. It is not absolutely certain but only highly probable that the employee has actually embezzled the money. Since, however, such "high probability" is not yet sufficiently sure to warrant its use in banking matters, the manager will put to his employee a series of careful and perpetrating questions. He will ask him on what day the sum in question was embezzled; whether he made false entries into the books; how they were made, etc. Finally, he will have the books gone over by a third person. Thus his "belief" is confirmed. The actuality of the embezzlement which he "believed" from the first moment has been established.

Nonetheless this *scientia testimonialis*, which we will call pseudo-faith from now on, is completely different in its structure from faith in the proper sense. This becomes evident if we compare pseudo-faith with faith in the proper sense in a phenomenological reflection upon both. Let us assume that a bank employee was convicted of embezzlement by reason of more or less weighty circumstantial evidence. The police, the judge and also the general public are convinced of his guilt. He maintains that, to the contrary, he is innocent. And his wife, who loves him with her whole heart, believes him; she has faith in him. She has made no investigation of her own; she has gathered no evidence. She simply believes him in the face of all arguments to the contrary.

If we compare this belief with the example adduced above of *scientia testimonialis*, we see that we can justly call the one faith and the other pseudo-faith. In one instance we are dealing with a completely impersonal, purely objective calculation of probabilities which is finally experienced as "practical certainty." For if the probability is so great that the opposite is practically excluded, then one is "practically certain." This is pseudo-faith, which enjoys no greater certitude than that possessed by its many logical premises. In the other instances however we find a highly personal, completely unobjective act of knowledge, placed in the face of all the objective evidence, and which to all appearance is "illogical." Furthermore the certitude of this act is out of proportion to the certainty of its possible premises. It is more certain "than we can logically account for." A second difference also meets the eye. In pseudo-faith the object of assent, the object of the act of knowledge, is the assertion alone. Pseudo-faith is a mere holding as true of a definite assertion on the ground of a more or less certain calculation concerning the value of its evidence. Faith, on the contrary, has as its object the entire person, who as the bearer of the assertion is accepted along with it. In pseudo-faith we say "all the circumstances point to his innocence"; in faith in the proper sense we say "Peter is a good man."

One might object here that the difference between faith and pseudo-faith is an illusion. In reality we find only the element which we call pseudo-faith. What we call faith is merely a "borderline case" which is particularly striking because of its irrationality. Really however there is only one structure—that of pseudo-faith—which can have different grades of rationality and awareness. This objection must be considered seriously. The two kinds of faith are frequently confused, and not without reason, for there are actually many instances in which one man places an act of faith and another an act of pseudo-faith. One man "believes" the newspaper; the other estimates that in relation to this concrete news item, what the paper reports is, with great probability, the truth of the matter. One believes what a stranger says when the stranger gives him information of no greater consequences; the other says to himself: "In matters of such small importance the man most certainly is not going to lie to me." One student believes his professor; another says to himself: "In such a matter which can be checked with relatively little difficulty he cannot afford to say what is not so." Furthermore it happens quite frequently that we believe a man on first acquaintanceship, and then all at once find ourselves calling into question his ethical integrity. The very next minute we no longer believe him but rather decide through a sort of calculation that, nonetheless, what he is saying is most probably the truth in this particular instance. We should not be surprised then that people have attempted to put faith and pseudo-faith on the same level. These instances however are merely "borderline cases." And borderline cases are never a valid norm, even if they be numerous. We willingly admit that this borderline area where faith and pseudo-faith can over-lap is a wide one. This should not lead us, however, to an oversimplification which would do violence to the phenomena. Whatever we may say of them in terms of meta-physics of cognition, it is clear that, viewed phenomeno-logically, faith is distinct from pseudo-faith. No matter how uncomfortably and seemingly "illogical" the act of faith may be, we still cannot equate it in a phenomenologi-cal reflection with pseudo-faith without at the same time doing violence to the phenomena. We need only to con-sider the more significant examples of faith and pseudo-faith to see that they are fundamentally different in their phenomenological structure. This difference can be sche-matically represented as follows:

	Faith	Pseudo-Faith
Object:	the concrete person plus the assertion	the assertion alone
Certitude:	for the most part greater than the possible prior knowledge	as strong as the prior knowledge, from which the syllogism arises

This difference becomes even clearer if we consider more closely the most significant example of faith—the faith which unites people who love each other. If I believe the words of a person whom I love very much, then this person becomes a second "I." I take him just as he is and place myself within his "I." He has become my "I"; he takes my place; he becomes my representative. The non-identity which exists between us is surpassed somehow on a higher level. Without ceasing to be myself, I become identical with him, with his total "I," with his concrete historical "I." That I believe him merely means that I accept and recognize this Thou in its total singularity. This faith is fundamentally nothing else than the cognitive correlative of love. Indeed, love is love in the true sense only insofar as it is coupled with this faith. This cognitive acceptance of the Thou as a concrete whole is the fundamental element of personal faith.

If this person now reveals himself to me, if he opens up his innermost self to me and allows me to enter into his interiority by word and sign, if he tells me he loves me, then I put my faith in his assertion. For this statement is, precisely insofar as it is considered as a statement, a partial element of the concrete Thou. The Thou to which I assent and which I acknowledge is not merely an abstract substantial substratum but the concrete Thou in its entirety: the whole person with his entire past which has been taken up into the present moment, with these individual eyes of his, who exists and reveals himself to me as the concrete individual he is and nothing else. His assertion is a peripheral element, it is an expression of this existential totality; and I say "yes" to his assertion and accept it because I have said "yes" to him as a whole.

Here we see most clearly the difference between faith and pseudo-faith. In pseudo-faith a statement is held to be true on the basis of logical reasoning. This holding-to-be-true of a statement is simply an explicit or implicit syllogism which is no more certain or uncertain than its premises. "I know that he is not lying now; I hear and understand what he is saying to me; and therefore I accept it as true." This

holding-to-be-true of a statement is by no means a personal
act. I do not here say "yes" to a human Thou in his dignity
and singularity. The Thou is here really superfluous, for we
test the veracity of the needle on a gauge or a speedometer
in exactly the same way we are testing it here.

A second fact becomes still clearer now than it has been
heretofore. The essential core of the act of faith is the "yes"
spoken to the concrete Thou and not the accompanying
assent given to his assertion. The object of the act of faith
is therefore primarily the concrete Thou, and only secondarily his assertions. If I really personally believe a person then I place an act of assent and approval directed
toward this person as such. Only on the ground of this
"yes" which I say to him do I accept his assertions as true.
In the personal act of faith there is contained therefore a
twofold object: the concrete Thou and his statements.
The latter belong as a peripheral element to this concrete
Thou. These two elements do not stand side by side in
complete equality; they are organically structured. The
total personality's acceptance of the Thou is the fundamental, basic element; the acceptance of his assertions is
the peripheral element flowing from the first one. The
acceptance of the Thou, which is primary, leads me to the
point where I assent to his assertions and this means that I
consider them true. We must therefore, when we speak
of the object of the act of faith, separate the "Thou-belief"
and the "assertion-belief." Nonetheless we must always
remain aware of the fact that, although both elements can
be distinguished, they can never be separated. For faith
which would merely have an assertion for its object would

no longer be faith but a pseudo-faith, an act of *scientia testimonialis*. And faith which would have only a person and not his assertions and self-revelation as its object could never be a "yes" spoken to the person in his totality, in his total historical existentiality, for although his statements are indeed peripheral, they are still an element which pertains essentially to this concrete and historical unicity.

3   The Object and Certitude of Faith

According to the person toward whom the act of faith is directed the certainty as well as the object of personal faith can differ very greatly, and so also in consequence can faith itself. There are numerous levels of personal faith. We have faith in our parents, our friends, our acquaintances, our children, and even persons whom we do not know. The certitude and the object of our faith are quite different, depending on the profundity of these personal relationships and upon the person in whom we place our faith. We can nonetheless distinguish three fundamental forms of personal faith: faith in our friends, faith in our acquaintances, and faith in people who are unknown to us. We could, obviously, distinguish several levels of faith, for the shades of distinction are manifold. For our purposes however a simple threefold division suffices. But there is no question here of essential differences, rather one simply of different levels of belief.

1. *Faith in Strangers.*

If I ask a stranger the way to a certain street, and if I "put my faith" in his answer, I have elicited a personal act.

I have, to be sure, encountered a stranger, yet I treat him
for what he is, a person. I ask him, listen to his answer,
accept it and am grateful for the information which he
gives me. I believe what he says.

One will be inclined here perhaps to call the personal
nature of this act into question. Do we really have a personal act here? Or is it not rather an act of pseudo-faith
or an implicit syllogism which we might formulate more or
less as follows? Man as such is worthy of belief. This
stranger is a man. Therefore he is worthy of belief. The
general knowledge we possess of a person as such is applied
to an individual person through an implicit syllogism. As a
matter of fact however we have no experience of such an
implicit syllogism, and it can be questioned whether it
makes sense to interpret this natural and highly spon-
taneous movement of our intellect as some form of implicit syllogism. We are not dealing here with discursive,
conceptual thought but with a concrete intuition. If I
believe a stranger, I don't think according to this or that
conceptual process. I "see" that this stranger is worthy
of belief and I believe what he says. There is nothing here
to suggest a conceptual process, and every syllogism—
even an implicit syllogism—is a conceptual process. If
the expression "implicit syllogism" can be said to have a
meaning, it must mean that this type of knowledge, although it is not consciously perceived as logical reasoning,
is nonetheless present to consciousness at least as conceptual
thought. Otherwise one would be forced to say that every
intuition, even the artistic intuition, is merely an "implicit
syllogism." Yet the precise point to be noted in the ex-

ample we have given is that in it no conceptual knowledge is present; that is, no universal concept precisely as universal. If I meet a stranger, I do not think about a "man." We do not "think" in this case at all; we simply believe the man. One might describe this phenomenon as follows. If I believe a stranger, I believe him because every encounter with a stranger is already a "personal intuition" from which the act of belief springs, as it were, spontaneously. This and this alone is manifested in a phenomenological reflection on the phenomenon. And we have, for the time being at least, no right to characterize this phenomenon as "merely syllogistic." Characterizations which go beyond the descriptions of phenomena are out of place at this point in our inquiry.

Whether we are permitted to characterize this operation as an "implicit syllogism" or not is therefore a question which must remain unanswered for the present. Undoubtedly we are confronted here with a phenomenon in the personal sphere. However reserved may be the commitment which is made here, it is still an essentially personal one. We do not give ourselves completely to a stranger, nor do we surrender ourselves to one entirely. Nevertheless some sort of self-giving, some personal surrender is present. For to place our faith in a stranger is nothing else than to see a certain object through his eyes. What we do not know from personal experience, we know nonetheless because we experience it through the stranger's eyes. This is a placing-of-ourselves-in-the-standpoint-of-the-other; it is a certain committing of ourselves. If we understand love as our total commitment to a "thou," this faith is not love. Yet love is an analogous concept, whose extension is very broad. Some type of love is surely present here as well. Proof for this is found in the fact that every stranger feels hurt if we do not believe him in matters of small importance. He expects that I will show him some measure of esteem and love. I too feel that I must show my love for him through some small sign—the love which is expressed in my words of thanks for the information I have received from him.

This personal faith in a stranger plays a large role in our interpersonal relationships. Without it life would be almost impossible. This is the way in which we have faith in a person whom we meet on the street or in the workman to whom we entrust the execution of a task. Or again, consider for a moment the modern news media, radio stations, newspapers, books, etc. They inform us of matters of fact which in most cases we could theoretically verify, if we had the time and the necessary means, or of which we could learn from many other people. Since people cannot actually verify these facts, at least as a general rule, they take them on faith from newspapers, books or television. This faith is, as will be shown later, and as we have now discovered through our phenomenological analysis, a legitimate form of belief without which people could no longer lead a human life.

This faith which one places in strangers is limited however to certain objects. We believe a stranger for the most part only about matters of no great moment. We believe him if he speaks of matters of common knowledge, or if what he says presents no great difficulty, i.e. if it can easily be verified. But it is characteristic of all these cases that only objective data constitute the object of our belief. These communications in which we put our faith are mostly concerned with the objective world, with the world of everyday experience, with technical matters or with public affairs. If a stranger communicates to us his most intimate plans, fears or anxieties, or some deeply personal event in his life, we find this "shocking," and generally refuse to believe what he says. We could say therefore that, generally speaking, it is not profound personal revelations which constitute the object of this kind of faith but rather impersonal data which possess no great importance.

The certitude attached to such belief is also very slight. For as soon as the suspicion is aroused on any ground whatsoever that the state of the case may be otherwise, we no longer believe a stranger. As soon as we learn that this person is no longer completely worthy of belief, we attempt to verify the facts. The certitude of this kind of faith is experienced as one of the lowest degrees of certitude. It is genuine certitude of course, but certitude of the lowest grade. Therefore we generally believe strangers only in unimportant, impersonal matters, and this faith is endowed with no great certitude.

2. *Belief between Acquaintances.*

The belief which we place in our acquaintances is considerably deeper and more personal. The object of belief here embraces personal facts and actions. The certitude of faith is in this case much greater than is the faith which people place in strangers. If I make an intimate personal revelation to a person whom I know well and he promises me that he will tell no one, I believe what he says. I would not act this way however with a stranger. I can tell in confidence to a man whom I know well things which I would never mention to a stranger. I believe that he will be understanding and that he will never do anything to harm me. I also believe an acquaintance if he tells me he needs help badly, but we can hardly be expected to believe a stranger in such a case. Perhaps we can conclude from his dress that he is in need but this is surely not belief.

I also have acquaintances whom I do not believe. If I know that a person always deceives me or at least attempts to deceive me or if I know that he does not even tell the truth in unimportant matters because he wants to play tricks with me, then I will not put my faith in him. If I know a man well, and if I know that his tendency is to lie in business affairs, then I do not trust him in such matters. This knowledge I have of him is the cause of my "not believing." But this "not believing" is essentially different from the nonbelief that I show toward a stranger. For one case involves a personal act of nonbelief which arises from definite knowledge. I know that this person is not worthy of belief. In the other case we are dealing with nonbelief which is caused simply by not-knowing. I do not believe a man because I do not know him well enough to do so, or because he is a total stranger to me.

In such cases too belief or nonbelief can be more or less profound and personal. If the object of my belief is restricted here, this is because the content of my knowledge of an acquaintance conditions the object of my belief. According to the knowledge I have concerning an acquaintance, I will believe him only in certain matters or I will not believe him at all. If however we prescind from the content of our knowledge of an acquaintance and consider only the purely formal structure of this kind of faith, we can say that as a rule we believe acquaintances not only about matters of small moment or about purely objective facts, but also where personal matters are concerned. In other words, the faith which one puts in an acquaintance embraces a more profound and personal dimension. The object of belief is much more personal in this case than in the faith we place in strangers. Here a new element enters the picture: the content of this knowledge of the man whom I encounter conditions also my belief, a fact which will be the object of further inquiry.

The certitude of the faith which people put in acquaintances is also considerably greater than the certainty of faith put in strangers. If a stranger says to me that he saw my friend X in city Y, I believe him. But if a man whom I know well tells me that he has been in conversation with the friend in city Z, I will no longer believe the stranger but rather the man who is well known to me. As a general rule therefore, this type of faith possesses a higher degree of certitude.

This is the type of faith we put in the multitude of people with whom we deal in our daily life. To show clearly its importance we need only say that the body of knowledge which we receive in school, in the university and from the publication of scholarly research is grounded for the most part on this faith.

In these cases too faith is combined with a kind of esteem

and love—that type of love which people in everyday language call acquaintanceship and which finds expression as sympathy, esteem, helpfulness or just plain friendliness.

We have also seen that in faith between acquaintances not only the object of faith, but also its certitude is more personal than in faith between strangers. We find in the former in contrast to belief between strangers a greater personal depth. We indicated also, in passing as it were, that the act of faith, the commitment of the total person to a Thou as a concrete totality, does not in every case mean that a person must accept absolutely all the elements of this Thou unconditionally, i.e. all his physical and moral deficiencies. We can assent to a person fully, but as a general rule we assent with definite restrictions. We accept him with the explicit or implicit exception of some definite moral deficiency. I can, for example, accept a friend as a total human person without giving my approval to certain failings which are still inherent in his nature. This fact conditions all those cases in which I accept a person and give him my approval through my faith in him without, nevertheless, accepting some of his statements. If I know, for example, that a man who is in other respects an upright person has a tendency to gross exaggeration in narrating his hunting experiences, I will give him my approval through belief, but with the exception of this area of his life. If he says to me that he needs help badly, I will believe what he says. If he says to me however that he did such and such on his last hunting expedition, I will smile and let it go at that. If I know a man of excellent character, but know that he tends to praise the qualities of his children to the skies, I will not believe him when he talks about his children or I will agree only with reservations. All these examples are typical and show clearly that we can accept a person fully and that we can through belief give our approval to his whole person without accepting a definite area of his personality (and correspondingly also his assertions).

Perhaps it might be objected here that this is not an acceptance of the Thou as a whole, therefore it is not belief. But we are conducting our inquiry along phenomenological lines and must consequently be directed by the phenomena. The phenomena are clear here. We can accept a person in his total concreteness and yet exclude, implicitly or explicitly, a certain dimension of his personality. It might be said that we accept that Thou in this case but not as a whole. Indeed not everything that ontically belongs to this Thou is accepted. We can nevertheless speak of an acceptance of the Thou as a whole to the extent that exclusion of a definite dimension takes place, as it were, only subsequently. When we speak of the acceptance of the Thou as a whole, we mean by this that we accept the Thou as a totality in and for itself. Therefore there is no question of the acceptance of a man insofar as he is an expert or an official or a politician, but the acceptance of the TOTAL person. That belief however is the acceptance of the whole person in and for itself does not mean always that we can exclude certain areas per accidens. The act of belief has, accordingly, as its object the concrete person as a whole. Per accidens however it can happen that because of our prior knowledge of a person, we will exclude from the whole to which we give our acceptance and approval the area which is the object of this prior knowledge.

Every act of belief is a personal act and as such is directed to a Thou. This Thou, which is the object of the act of belief, is a personal Thou, a person and therefore a total entity. Just as the personal admits of degrees, so too does this "total entity." In belief between strangers a Thou and therefore a whole is assented to. That the assent given to the Thou as a total entity is relatively superficial is shown by the fact that we do not unconditionally accept all his assertions. The personal which is always a total entity is, as a whole of course, still only partially the object of a relatively superficial assent or approbation. In the faith between acquaintances this total entity is revealed in a new and deeper way.

3. *Faith between Friends.*

Faith between intimate friends is the culmination of interpersonal faith. It is an unconditional commitment to a Thou, to whom we give our complete trust and whom we love from the bottom of our hearts. This faith includes a loving, self-forgetting, unreserved, approving "yes" spoken to the other. We have here an unconditional approbation given to the whole human personality of a Thou.

The object of faith embraces in this instance not only a given area of life, but simply every area. Nothing is excluded from it. In the center of the object of faith however is found the personal element, particularly the self-revelations of the Thou. We believe this or that about a person whom we love, but our faith in him reaches its deepest level when his communication to us reveals his innermost self. Therefore it is characteristic of this type of faith that through it our faith touches not any given statement so much as the entire person. The total person is given our unreserved approval for his own sake. This is why the certitude of this type of faith is so great. Everything a mere acquaintance says cannot be believed without reservation, whether he speaks of himself, his future plans, his inclinations and aversions, or his most intimate feelings. This is even truer when what he says is most improbable. A person whom we love however can be believed, or rather must be believed, in everything he says. And in this simple act of faith we are aware of an unshakeable certitude. In it alone do we feel utterly secure. It will take a long time to convince the wife whose husband is convicted of a serious crime that he is really guilty, if she has his word to the contrary and if she really loves him with all her heart. Perhaps she will never believe that he is guilty, and this in spite of all the evidence opposed to her belief. The certitude of this type of faith is so great that often even self-evident arguments are unable to shake it.

Thus it is shown phenomenologically that there exists a gradation in personal faith. The object of faith and consequently the certitude of its conviction differ according to the depth of the interpersonal relations from which the act of faith arises. The knowledge which I possess of a person and the greater or lesser degree of love which I have for him condition both the object of faith and its certitude. Therefore we must study more carefully the personal knowledge which precedes faith to see how it conditions the act of faith itself. How and to what extent the object and

certitude of belief are intrinsically dependent upon one
another, and how "Thou-belief" and "assertion-belief" condition one another, are questions which will have to be
discussed again when we approach our problem from the
angle of the metaphysics of knowledge.

4   Faith and Personal Knowledge

If we say that the depth of personal faith, that is, the
object and certainty of faith, is conditioned by a knowledge
which precedes faith in the proper sense, then this statement does not appear to be sufficiently accurate. For we
should really, so it seems, enlarge on this formulation and
say that personal faith is conditioned by a not-knowing
which is prior to faith. The faith which we place in a
stranger appears to be conditioned by not-knowing rather
than by positive knowledge. I believe a stranger not precisely
because I know anything about him but rather because
he is a stranger and therefore really because I do not know
him. However this is not actually the case. For a mere
not-knowing is a purely negative reason and a purely negative reason is actually no reason at all. It is rather the negation of a reason. A negation as such can never be the
reason why we perform a positive act. If we maintain therefore that we believe a stranger because we see no reason why
we should not believe, then this presupposes that there
must be a real, even though less positive reason why we
should believe him at all. If we say that we believe a
stranger "to such a slight degree" or "very superficially"
simply because he is a stranger, then this means that ab-

sence of knowledge about this person is the negative ground for the purely negative state of affairs which is implied in the expression "to such a slight degree." "To such a slight degree" however implies a positive state of affairs as well. We believe a stranger "to a slight degree" but still and all we believe him. And for this positive state of affairs a positive reason must be given. The knowledge prior to belief concerning a man whom we believe is therefore presupposed for faith placed in a stranger. We must examine this knowledge more carefully. It will be shown that it is not any type of knowledge at all but a genuine personal knowledge.

We do not know much about strangers. But if we can believe a stranger, it is only because we already know what man is and because we encounter him as a person. We know that he is a spiritual being, that he is a person; and we know that a person as such is worthy of belief. As a general principle men do not lie. On the contrary, their nature inclines them to tell the truth. Man's mind is ordered to truth and this natural inclination makes man as such trustworthy. We can believe a stranger because we know already that man as such is trustworthy. Since however the stranger that we encounter in the real order is not "man as such," he is not simply and unconditionally trustworthy. He could be a depraved individual quite capable of deceiving his fellow men. For this reason we believe this man only about matters of no consequence and objective facts of no importance which can easily be verified.

That personal knowledge precedes the faith which we place in our acquaintances is so evident that it hardly calls

for proof. For it is clear that this personal knowledge conditions faith and if it conditions it, it must precede it. If,
for example, we know a person well and realize that he is
inclined to lie about money matters, then we do not have
faith in him in this regard; but we do when he speaks about
other matters. Here also there is personal knowledge prior
to faith in the proper sense which conditions the act of faith
itself in respect to its content and its certitude.

What exactly is this personal knowledge? Why have we
called this knowledge which precedes faith and conditions
it "personal knowledge"? In what manner does this personal knowledge condition the act of faith?

Let us turn our attention to the faith which forms the
bond between intimate friends. The structure of the personal knowledge prior to faith is much more evident here
than it is in the faith which we place in other men. This
structure is really the same in every type of faith. Here
however it is so clearly in the foreground that we can
recognize it readily. To become better acquainted with the
structure of faith and personal knowledge, we will not
consider "borderline" cases but rather that case where it is
in evidence most clearly and in no uncertain terms.

Knowledge prior to the act of faith, when faith is the
bond between intimate friends, is extremely subtle and
complex in structure. This is obvious in the extreme difficulty we experience in describing or in clearly characterizing an intimate friend. If we ask someone about a friend
of his, or ask what kind of a person this friend really is, he
finds himself quite at a loss for words. He knows his friend
very well indeed, and he is deeply attached to him. Truly

it is for this very reason that he cannot express what he knows in words, even if he is an experienced author. He knows his friend so well that to describe him at all appears at first sight quite impossible. If he tries to describe his friend, he realizes how jejune his description is, how color-less are his concepts, and how inexact is the information he is giving. The extent and depth of personal knowledge in a case like this becomes therefore the reason for a kind of inability to express its contents adequately in judgments and in concepts. If then this kind of personal knowledge, whose content is so rich, really exists, and if we cannot adequately express it in judgments and in concepts, what is this personal knowledge after all? Is it a concept, or a judg-ment composed of several concepts, or is it perhaps merely an image derived from sense perception? It is none of these. This personal knowledge is not given in experience as a concept or as a conceptual judgment, nor as a purely sensible image, since there are many things which we know about a friend and which cannot be represented in the phantasm. There is always more to personal knowledge than the phantasm can contain. If personal knowledge were merely a concept or a judgment, we could adequately express it through concepts and judgments, at least in its essential elements. But this is not the case. If personal knowledge is neither concept nor judgment nor sense knowl-edge, what then can it be? We experience it as an intuition. It is—in contrast to the judgment—a single unity, in which there is no distinction between subject and predicate. It is a purely intellectual "image" which presents to the mind a whole object in a single unity. It is a knowledge which—

in contrast to the concept and to any type of sense knowledge—is aware of its own truth (*continet veritatem
formalem*).

I know a person. I look into his eyes. I shake his hand.
My senses convey to me a whole series of observations.
Generally speaking, however, we do not direct our attention to the activity of the senses. I look into his eyes and
from the light I see in them I know, to some extent at
least, who he is. I see his smile, hear his words, and my
mind consciously or half-unconsciously takes in all those
little details that make up our objective and unobjective
knowledge of another. Slowly I fill in the bare outline of the
image I had formed of him at the time of our first encounter. This intellectual image grows richer, more vivid
as times goes by. Subtle lights and shadows make their
appearance. The longer I deal with this person, the richer
in content grows my image of him. And—this is typical
of the experience—I find that I can no longer express my
knowledge conceptually. Concepts are too abstract, color-
less and inexact. My intellectual image now so rich and
finely shaded has become transconceptual. Concepts can
no longer express its fullness. At the outset of my acquaintanceship with this person I might still perhaps have thought
it possible to express this intellectual image in some conceptual form or other, even though my attempt to do so was
not entirely successful. When I get to know him well, very
well, this clearly is no longer possible. My personal knowledge, my intuition has transcended the realm of conceptual expression. To put it more exactly, although my
personal knowledge was always intuitive and therefore trans-

conceptual, this fact has now become more than ordinarily evident. If, for example, I say during my first encounter with a person: "He has a steely way of looking at you," this judgment has already present within it the tension between concept and intuition. I can express with these concepts the fact that he has a "steely look," but the full significance of this concept "steely look" can be understood only by someone who knows what "steely look" is through his own intuition. The content of the concept comes from the intuition in the first place. The concept is an aspect abstracted from the intuition. During my first encounter with this man I did not realize how deep was the intuition which led me to make this statement. Later on however I come to realize that he really has a "look like steel" and I realize also how little this concept expresses of what I really mean. The structure of personal knowledge therefore has always been such that it could not be expressed in concepts. This type of knowledge then cannot be simply designated as another form of conceptual thought; nor can it be reduced to it. In experience it appears to us as prior to conceptual knowledge. First we have personal knowledge of a man; then we try to express this knowledge somehow in conceptual form.

For the present we should refrain from giving any definite philosophical meaning to the expression "intuition," for we are pursuing here a purely phenomenological analysis. In this context we mean by intuition, in contrast to concept and to conceptual thought, concrete knowledge which brings us in contact with the concrete as such, which is aware of its own conformity to reality (*continet veritatem*

formalem) and which is present to consciousness as a single
unity (without separation of subject and predicate). This
consciousness is in large part unobjective; i.e. it is a genuine
and true knowledge, but still knowledge which is not entirely present to consciousness as "an object." Its limits
become progressively obscure and almost incomprehensible
until they finally disappear. It is knowledge of which we
can give no account; it is the knowledge which Augustine
speaks of when he writes: "Unasked, we know it; if we
are asked, we no longer know it." This is the phenomenon
of personal knowledge prior to faith. It is an intuition of a
Thou which is to a great extent unobjective. Speaking in
purely phenomenological terms we can say no more than
we have. On the other hand however we can say no less.

People might perhaps object that this personal knowledge, this intuition is already faith in the proper sense. Yet
such an opinion would be false. For I can have such a personal intuition of an inveterate and vicious liar and still I
do not believe him, and the very reason why I refuse to
believe him is because I have such personal knowledge of
him. I can have dealings with a person for many years
and possess a very finely structured personal knowledge of
him; yet it is still quite possible that I am less ready to
believe him than a man who is just a casual acquaintance.
I have no love for him, nor will I place any trust in him as
I will in those to whom I give the approval of my faith. We
can therefore have a relatively full personal knowledge of
man and still fail to believe him. Personal knowledge must
not therefore be equated with faith. If a determined type
of personal knowledge is not coincident with faith but

precedes it, we cannot say that every type of personal knowledge must be equated with belief. If this is the case then there is no reason why we could not accept without hesitation the testimony of consciousness that personal knowledge is distinct from faith in the proper sense and precedes it.

If one objects that this personal knowledge does not always precede faith, he is partly correct. For if I meet a person and speak with him, I have already begun to believe him at this very first encounter. But this faith is also the type which we place in strangers. And previous to this faith, as we have already shown, is genuine personal knowledge even though it be of a superficial type. From this sort of human intercourse and from this type of faith gradually arises a deeper personal knowledge and this conditions in its turn a deeper faith. From this arises further a new and deeper intuition which again makes possible an even more profound faith. This mutual conditioning does not militate against the position we have been maintaining but merely refines it: prior to every type of faith is found a grade of personal knowledge corresponding to it.

If we now ask how the intuition conditions the object and the truth of faith, we find ourselves in a rather difficult position. For the simple observation of the phenomenon merely shows us that one rises from the other. How this happens we do not "see." Some things however can be accepted as phenomenologically proven. It has been shown, for example, that the content of the intuition plays a large role in this area. There is no question here merely of a "syllogistic dependence," for in the syllogism the conclusion is no surer than the least certain premise (*pejorem semper sequitur conclusio partem*). But this is not so here. For I can have an extremely certain intuition of a person and nevertheless believe him only to a slight degree. Nevertheless the content of the intuition has still a large role to play. It is precisely because my extremely certain intuition reveals this man to me as completely unworthy of belief that I have no faith in him.

We know very little about the logical connection which exists between intuition and the act of faith. We will return to this aspect in the course of our inquiry into the metaphysics of cognition. But we can already even at this point consider one thing as proven: the simple proportion "the larger A is, the greater will be B" cannot be validly applied to intuition and to faith. The certitude of the intuition is not always proportioned to the certitude of the act of faith.

5 Faith as a Personal Attitude

In the previous section we have already considered the difference between intuition and belief. Now we must still briefly examine another problem. What is the determining element that makes faith in the proper sense faith? How should the act of faith as such be characterized in contrast to other types of knowledge? How is faith in a definite person different from an intuition which has this particular person for its content?

We have already seen that the act of faith cannot be placed on the same level as concepts, judgments and syllogisms. There is, to be sure, also a "faith-proposition," that is, a conceptual expression, which contains the word "believe." "I believe that you will help me." But we already know that this "faith-proposition" is a secondary phenomenon. It is merely the conceptual and discursive explication or analysis of faith in the proper sense, which however is not itself of a conceptual or discursive nature. Just as a proposition is merely an explication of the intuition, the "evidence" which precedes it and underlies it, so the faith-proposition is nothing other than the conceptual or discursive analysis of the act of faith.

What then is the act of faith? Is it merely the intuition which we have of a concrete person? Certainly belief is intuitive in nature. It is knowledge which presents an object to a knower in its concreteness with no separation of subject and predicate. But the act of faith is nonetheless different in its structure from intuition.

The phenomenological difference between the act of faith and intuition cannot be determined through the reference we make to the content of both. Not only the act of faith but the intuition considered in the previous section have the concrete historical person for their content. Not only can I have an intuition of Peter, I can also have real faith-knowledge of him. Both are intuitive types of knowledge which represent Peter in his historical concreteness. We can therefore set up no phenomenological distinction between the two.

If we compare the act of belief to the intuition however, even though both have as their content the historical Peter, the phenomenological difference becomes evident. The act of faith is not, as is the intuition, simply knowledge of an

objectively given human Thou; it is in addition a free
attitude toward this Thou adopted by our whole person.
Or to put it more exactly: the act of faith is the cognitive
element of a free, fully personal attitude of one whole
person toward another person in his historical concreteness.

If I believe Peter, this act of belief is not merely knowledge of what Peter is in himself objectively, but more than
that it embodies also my personal attitude toward him. In
believing Peter, I accept him. Belief always means not
simply knowledge, but more than that a personal acceptance
and approval of human Thou.

The phenomena are unambiguously clear in this respect.
For I can have an intuition of a person which is extremely
rich in content without its being necessarily and always
faith or its refusal. In the early stages of personal knowledge,
I can grasp a person intuitively without taking a stand
toward him as a whole personality. I neither accept nor
reject him as a person. I am satisfied with the objective
knowledge of this Thou. The moment however that I
either accept or reject him through personal commitment,
I transform this cold, objective intuition into a personal act
of faith or its refusal.

The act of faith therefore is distinct from the intuition to
the extent that it always implies a personal attitude. The
object of the act of belief is not merely "known"; it becomes
the object of my personal acceptance or rejection. This
acceptance or rejection moreover is not an objectively encountered action but a deliberate personal relationship.
Faith is therefore always knowledge and acceptance. This
personal relationship is deliberately brought into being

in the framework of an attitude of the total personality. From this it follows that the act of faith more than any other form of knowledge is closely connected with our personal center and therefore with our free will. The most proper and specific element of the act of faith consequently consists in the fact that the intuition of a Thou is the cognitive element of a total attitude of our whole person toward this Thou. In this fact we find the distinction which exists between the act of faith and intuition and every other form of knowledge.

6   The Three Levels of Knowledge

So far our considerations have led us to a distinction between three levels of human knowledge. This section will present a synthetic outline of these degrees of knowledge, indicating their relation to each other and the lines of demarcation between them. This can best be done by a phenomenological reflection on the three degrees of knowledge, using one significant example without delaying over fine shadings and borderline cases. The three degrees are conceptual thought, intuition and personal knowledge as faith. It should be borne in mind that the method employed in this section is always purely phenomenological. If then we distinguish the three degrees of knowledge, we intend this distinction to be purely phenomenological. Whether and to what extent we can make such a distinction from the point of view of a metaphysics of cognition is a question which will concern us later.

The dawning of human knowledge takes place in an

intuition. I see and hear a concrete man. This dawn of knowledge is a single, undivided image of the man. I do not first see his head, then his hands, finally his legs, and so through the addition of all these parts see the whole person. The phenomena here are absolutely clear. I see first the whole person and only in retrospect do I concentrate my attention on his head, his hands or the other portions of his body. Even in cases in which I see at first only a person's face, I still see him as a total person. For the individual, sense impressions are always grasped, even in this early dawn of intellectual knowledge, as a whole. Our problem at the moment is not to determine to what extent this first image of a man is sense or intellectual knowledge. Both elements are experienced simultaneously as constituents of one total image. It is important for us to note here that the beginning of the intellectual cognition takes place in an "image," in an intuition. I see Peter in his concreteness, with his eyes, and with his own determined way of acting. This "image," this intuition is not a concept. Neither is it a judgment, or a syllogism. The evidence of our phenomenological reflections forbids its reduction to conceptual thinking. It is concrete, not abstract. It is an undivided unity, not a combination of subject and predicate. This simple, undivided image of the concrete man Peter we call an intuition. Whether another name should be given to it from the point of view of the metaphysics of knowledge need not concern us here. Phenomenologically the intuition of the concrete man (or thing) is the beginning of intellectual knowledge. It is therefore most important to observe that this first degree of intellectual knowledge appears to consciousness incorporated in a sensible phantasm (*in phantasmatibus*).

The analytic mind then abstracts from the fullness of this concrete intuition one determined aspect. Thus arises the concept. The concept is an aspect abstracted from the intuition and so considered in itself. I can abstract from the intuition which I have formed of the concrete man Peter either the aspect "rationale" or the aspect "animal," or even "upright man" or "self-possessed personality." Now if I pair these concepts together and relate them to reality, I form the judgment: "Peter is a self-possessed personality." So the original intuition is progressively analyzed. From the intuition my conceptual knowledge of Peter takes its origin.

This conceptual knowledge, which consists of concepts and judgments, reacts upon the intuition which contains a new clarity and evidence. Through my analysis of the intuition I begin to discover how rich it has really been all along. Concepts and judgments therefore are simply an analysis of intuition. This analysis moreover leads to another synthesis to the extent that concepts and judgments disappear, as it were, from consciousness and are integrated into a purer and more luminous intuition. Intuition is thus seen to be the point of departure as well as the final stage of conceptual thought. Thus we have now outlined the first two levels of knowledge and their properties: the level of intuition and the level of conceptual knowledge (concept, judgment and syllogism).

It is self-evident that a vital circle is being formed here. Each time that I know Peter in a new situation my intuition of him is enriched through a new element. This new element gives an impetus to new conceptual and judgmental analyses and statements. This analysis reverts to synthesis, as it were, to the extent that the intuition embraces everything again in an undivided, concrete unity. Thus I come to know and appreciate Peter. But my knowledge of this man Peter has been up to now—let us say for the sake of argument—not personal. I knew him for what he really is: a person, a good man, etc. But there has been as yet no question of my taking a personal stand with regard to him. I have not yet accepted Peter into my personal life and as yet have neither accepted nor rejected him personally. I am still "objective" and personally uncommitted. This intuition shows me Peter as a good, trustworthy man, just as another intuition shows me that the window is open. It is a matter of a purely objective situation.

If however I now take a personal stand through a free decision of my will, then Peter enters my personal life. He is no longer a mere object but someone who is personally accepted or rejected. This is the third level of knowledge. On this level personal knowledge is to be found, for there is question here of more than purely objective cognition. The objection might be raised that an act of the will is really not knowledge. True, yet the decision of the will is not given to us in experience as a pure, blind act of the will but rather as a concrete act which contains a cognitive element. This cognitive element of the free decision comes into play when, through a decision of our whole personal center, we say "yes" to Peter in his full concrete personality. The cold, objective intuition has now entered in the personal sphere and has been transformed into an element of the free decision of the will. The purely objective intuition merely says what Peter is. If however it is plunged, so to speak, into the free decision of the will, then of its essence it says much more. It becomes rejection or acceptance by my whole personal center of the concrete man Peter; it becomes faith or the refusal of faith.

The intuition and the conceptual analyses which depend upon it and proceed from it are pure cognition. They are the media through which the knower acquires an "image" of what he knows. (The expression "image" is very inaccurate and open to misunderstanding. Still it is difficult to avoid using it.) The act of faith is more than pure knowledge. It is the personal acceptance of a Thou, and this goes beyond the objectivity of pure knowledge. It is not just an act of knowledge which grasps the existent merely in the intentional order; it is much more than that. It is an attitude of the total human person to this existent. Therefore the act of faith is never possible except as the cognitive element of a free decision.

To do justice to the phenomena then, we must distinguish three levels of knowledge. For intuition, conceptual-judgmental knowledge and personal knowledge cannot be explained as different guides of an act of knowledge whose fundamental structure remains the same. Although these levels are found to exist in a kind of intercommunication, nonetheless they differ from one another in their structure.

Let us continue however our analysis of the faith process. The intuition, which shows me Peter as a good, very upright individual, is absorbed into the personal sphere and taken up into my free decision. Thereupon Peter enters my personal life and I will either accept or reject him with my whole personal center. This attitude of my whole personal center, which comes into being in a free decision, is clearly a work of the will and of the understanding too. The total personal "yes" therefore has both a volitional and a cognitive aspect. This cognitive element of the "yes" pronounced by my whole personal center is the act of faith. It is the cognitive "yes" said to a concrete Thou. Since however what Peter says pertains to his concrete Thou as a peripheral element, then also the statements which he makes, albeit peripheral elements of my intuition of Peter, are included in the whole to whom I say "yes." I say my "yes" to them because they are partial elements and manifestations of this concrete person. Since saying "yes" to an assertion is the same as "holding-an-assertion-to-be-true," by saying "yes" to Peter through faith, I also hold his statements as true. The "holding-to-be-true" of his assertions is therefore nothing more than a peripheral element of my saying "yes" to his Thou.

But just as the intuition could be analyzed, just as the intuition can be dissected into concepts and judgments, so too in a similar manner the act of faith can be subjected to analysis. For the act of faith has the intuition as its content insofar as a personal "yes" is said to it in a free decision. The act of faith therefore is itself intuitive, which means that it is neither a concept nor a judgment. But if my mind analyzes the act of faith and abstracts a definite aspect, I can form concepts and judgments. Thus I can also say: "I believe Peter when he tells me this." This expression—discursive conceptual knowledge—is an analysis of what is contained in the act of faith itself. I have abstracted a definite aspect of my act of faith through analysis and considered it in itself. This is how the faith-proposition comes into being.

Now we are able also to understand the inner meaning of the different verbal formulations. If I say: "I have faith in Peter as a person," then I have isolated in my analysis through concepts and judgments the central element of the act of faith. If on the other hand I say: "I believe what Peter says," then that element which I have isolated is peripheral to the act of faith, viz. the acceptance of statements which are included in the concrete Thou to whom I say my "yes."

Now we are also able to show why the act of belief must always be preceded by some sort of previous knowledge. This foreknowledge is nothing other than an intuition of the concrete Thou. It is absolutely necessary, for without such an intuition we cannot make personal decisions. We would assume a personal attitude to nothing, and an attitude toward nothing is ultimately no attitude and no act at all. Now we can also explain under certain circumstances why a definite area of a person's life is excluded from our faith. If my intuition represents Peter as very upright in general but unreliable in his hunting tales, then this area of life is excluded, and toward it I can say no "yes." Therefore statements made in respect to it are not accepted. We now understand better why a person feels hurt when we shall not take his word in matters of no moment. For such an attitude of nonbelief is at the same time an attitude of our whole personal center toward his concrete Thou which has resulted in a personal decision to say "no" to him.

Our phenomenological reflection will have to be carried

further. We must look into the certitude of the act of faith and consider its properties and origins. These and other problems are still untouched. We will have to deal with them later. The fundamental characteristics of interpersonal faith outlined here are not intended to provide an exhaustive phenomenology of the act of faith. A whole book would be required to do that. This brief analysis is meant to do no more than to cast some light on our problem and to serve as an introduction to the next section of the book, in which the act of faith is discussed from the point of view of the metaphysics of knowledge.

3 THE METAPHYSICAL STRUCTURE OF INTERPERSONAL FAITH

1 Pre-Personal Knowledge

In the previous section we saw that a phenomenology of three distinct levels of spiritual knowledge is required, if we are to reach an understanding of personal faith. These three levels were abstract discursive thought, intuition and essentially personal knowledge. In this section our endeavor will be to discover the metaphysical ground of possibility for the different knowledge structures revealed in these various levels. We shall also try to show that a further extension of the method employed by the scholastic authors in dealing with the problem of knowledge will lead us to place the same question that we have been led to place through our own approach to the problem of knowledge. We must turn our attention then to the scholastic theory of abstraction; and our consideration of its metaphysical background, even though it must confine itself to the main outlines of the theory, will furnish us with the point of departure which we need for our further development.

A. Metaphysics of Abstraction

1. *The Question of Being.* Man asks questions. If he does
not ask about this or that definite existent, but about the
Being of the existent, he is engaged in metaphysics. All Being, even that of the questioner, comes under his inquiry.[24]

This question is ultimate. Only the absolute denial of
thought, which is impossible for man, could be more radical
than this question which embraces all knowledge, all objec-
tions, in a word, everything. If man chooses to ask about the
rationality, necessity or possibility of the Being-question,
then this newly formulated question would again be nothing other than the restatement of the question of Being. For
the question about individual things is only possible because man can ask about Being; and if he could not do so;
then the question about beings, insofar as they are such,
would be fundamentally impossible. For then he could only
ask about what in no wise existed, that is, about absolute
nothing; however a question about nothing is no question.
Therefore the question about Being manifests itself in its
fundamental originality as the transcendental condition of
possibility of any question whatever.[25]

If a man asks about the Being of an existent, he asks
about the undivided which unites the many individuals into
one whole. For a question about a part of Being is a question about its individuals; but this has, as we have already

[24] K. Rahner, *Geist in Welt*, 71–78. See also H. Rombach, "Über
Ursprung und Wesen der Frage: Symposion," *Jahrbuch für Philosophie*, vol. 3, Freiburg i. Br. 1952, 135–236.
[25] E. Coreth, *Metaphysik als Aufgabe*, 50–53.

shown, the Being-question as its transcendental condition of possibility. Therefore the Being which we ask about shows itself to be the undivided.[26]

If a man asks about the Being of an existent, he already knows what Being is. If man had absolutely no positive knowledge of Being, then his inquiry would be an empty and inconceivable absolute nothing; but since he asks about Being, he must necessarily know what Being is when he asks about it. But if man knows what Being is, then Being is knowable. The possibility of questioning Being reveals the possibility of knowing it.[27]

Being is not merely a possible question, but a necessary one. Since it must be questioned, since man, in asking about it, seeks dynamically an increase of his knowledge of Being, Being must be a possible goal of his tendential dynamism.[28] Undividedness, intelligibility and appetibility are therefore transcendental conditions of possibility for the metaphysical question, and so, also, transcendental attributes of Being.

Undividedness, intelligibility and appetibility are nevertheless relative determinations, for the negation of dividedness of actual knowledge and of actual striving for knowledge is essentially relative. Relation however means relatedness to something. Being therefore is characterized in a merely relative way through a duality. But this duality can only be understood in terms of the unity which makes it tran-

[26] K. Rahner, Geist in Welt, 70.

[27] K. Rahner, Geist in Welt, 72–74; Hörer des Wortes, 42–58.

[28] The mediation of the will which is indicated here will be discussed later at greater length. This will be done in the chapter on the personal reality.

scendentally possible. Therefore, if we want to express Being in itself, we must refer the relative attributes to their nonrelative positivity; Being is in itself and of itself not merely undividedness, intelligibility and appetibility, but unity, self-consciousness and self-will. If Being were not this, then it would contain potentiality, it would be in itself relative; it would not be the one Being of an existent, rather it would be itself a merely relative existent.

The absoluteness of Being will be expressed in merely formal terms; because Being is the principle of unity, self-knowledge and self-will, it is absolute as a *principium quo*. For that in virtue of which an existent is one, knows itself and others and is active, cannot be identical with that by which the existent is not one, not intelligent and not active.

2. *Existence and Essence.* Man is not absolute unity, absolute self-consciousness and absolute self-will. He asks about Being, but he is not himself that Being. And if man is not the absolute principle, then he must be one which is relative.[29] However he is not relative because he exists; otherwise Being would be in itself relative. If the basis of relativity is not Being, then it must be nonbeing, nothingness; not however absolute nothing, which can have no ground, but rather relative nothingness; but this merely pushes the question back a step. For how can relative nothingness be relative?

The relative can be positively determined since it is grasped as a relation to subsistent Being, which is not relative; the relative is the being that exists in essential relation

[29] The relative is the existent which is not identical with being itself. Therefore it is primarily relatively determined reality. It is not being.

to the absolute. But this is not enough. For the basis of relativity must be an intrinsic principle of the relative.[30] Relativity signifies duality; intrinsic relativity expresses a duality which is interior to the relative. If however a duality is interior to the relative, which makes possible its relativity, what is its nature? The Being that exists as its own Being is absolutely identical with itself and therefore not relative. Being is the absolute principle of unity. If something is relative, it cannot be absolutely identical with itself. The inner duality of the relative consists accordingly in this, that an element which does not exist as its own being is the principle of existence of the other, and that the other element which receives existence is the other of existence. The element that acts as existence [Sein] of the other is called existence. The other, that receives existence [Sein], we call essence. Essence and existence are the elements which constitute the internal ground of the relativity of beings.[31]

These elements are not relative in the same way. Existence, which gives being to essence, would, without the constituent connection with the essential element, no longer be existence, but the absolute principle of Being. Essence likewise would no longer exist if the principle of existence ceased to give it actuality; essence would become the mere possibility of a determined relationship with existence, and would therefore be a possible.

Of the constituents of the relative, existence reveals itself as that which gives actuality. As principle of actuality, it can

[30] This existent is not constituted simply by being, through which it is constituted an existent; it is also by another which is the ground of its nonidentity with being.
[31] E. Coreth, *Metaphysik als Aufgabe*, 66–70.

complete itself in essence without exhausting itself. The Being of the existent therefore "breaks through" the essence, overflows it and raises it to a new state of being. This Being of the existent, which breaks through the otherness of essence and completes itself in something new, we call activity.[32] Existence is the completion of essence; activity is its further completion, its *actus secundus*. If we call the totality of essence and existence "substance," and activities "accidents," we can then say, in summation: man, because he is a relative being, is composed of existence and essence, substance and accidents.

Through this composition of essence and existence, substance and accidents, the unity of the relative beings is partly dissolved; the unity becomes relative. If the unity of the relative beings is partly dissolved, then man's self-knowledge and self-will must in similar manner be relative. What kind of diminution is this? How is the self-knowledge and self-will of a relative being constituted?

Substance and accidents are not things or parts, but they are metaphysical constituents of the relative. Viewed metaphysically, self-knowledge and self-will are as much substance as accidents: metaphysics is not immediately empirical however, and therefore is not a datum of consciousness. The concrete whole alone is given empirically. Generally, the substance completing itself in accidents can be empirical presence to itself in self-knowledge and self-will. Empirical cognition and willing, in other words consciousness, are therefore immediately accidental but grounded in substance.

[32] E. Coreth, *Metaphysik als Aufgabe*, 59–62.

This metaphysical structure explains why a being is relative; it is the transcendental condition of possibility which allows man to ask a question at all about Being. But we have not yet reached the fundamental metaphysical structure of man. For the relative, which is composed of essence and existence, substance and accidents, has as its empirical consciousness self-knowledge and self-will. Indeed, such a being can also know the other, but its first knowledge, its *objectum proportionatum et proprium* is its own self. But this being is not man. Man is essentially directed to the other, and his first knowledge is not of his own self but of the other being. In other words, the metaphysical structure we have spoken of makes it clear how a being can be relative, and is therefore valid for all relative beings. If however this structure appears in a subject whose being is not weakened by any other kind of structure, then this subject is a pure spirit which, as such, has its own self as its first object of knowledge. Thus we have yet to show the structure that is peculiar to man.

3. *Matter and Form.* Cognition is nothing else than presence to oneself. For this reason it is primarily called self-knowledge.[33] Our cognition however is a receptivity which has the other as its first object of knowledge. How is this possible? Unity, cognition and willing are transcendental characteristics of being. They are not univocal, invariable quantities, but mutually correlative; the degree of a being's unity, cognition and willing corresponds to the degree of its actuality.

If a subject has the other as his first object of knowledge,

[33] K. Rahner, *Geist in Welt*, 80–90.

his own being must continually complete itself as "being-in-otherness." For if the knowing subject is limited by an other, then the other is the medium through which he realizes his presence to himself. What then is this other? It is not itself Being, for Being means self-knowledge and cannot therefore be the formal ground why the knowing subject is related to the other. This otherness must be a reality however, otherwise it would not be a real ground. If it is a reality, but not Being, it must be pure possibility for being. Only the pure other, the pure possibility of being is on the one hand real, but on the other hand not a being. Accordingly, it alone can be the medium in which the knowledge of the other exists: in the metaphysics of Thomas, it is called *materia prima*.

Man, who knows the other before he knows himself, possesses therefore an activity that is so immersed in the purely other that his own self becomes the selfness of the other. This dissolution [*Aufhebung*] of unity cannot consist merely in the activity itself, for the activity, since it is the activity of existence overflowing essence, carries within itself nothing but the fundamental determination of substance. If the unity of activity is weakened through a new otherness, then the unity of the substance is lessened in the same manner.

This new partial dissolution of its unity, which is intrinsic to the substance, must lie either in the principle of existence or in the essence. The principle of existence however is already in the otherness, in the essence. A further otherness is possible therefore only in the essence. The essence of a passively cognitive subject is, accordingly, one that is immersed in otherness. It contains two essential elements: its own essence and pure otherness. We call the first "form," the second "matter"; so the essence of man contains as its constituent elements form and matter. Matter is pure otherness, it is the otherness of otherness, pure possibility for being.

Knowledge of an other as one's first object of knowledge can only exist in a being whose principle of existence has been immersed through its own otherness (essence) in the otherness of the essence, where it now completes itself. If this knowledge tends to the other, we call it sense knowledge; if it turns back to the unity of its own self, it is called spiritual knowledge.

We can distinguish two elements of human understanding; the knowledge that tends to the other, and that which turns back upon itself (reditio completa ad seipsum). Two movements make this possible: one away from self and the other back to self. The movement "away from oneself" is not given a special name by tradition; the "turning back to oneself" is called "abstraction." The traditional teaching about abstraction takes its start therefore from knowledge of the other and sense knowledge, and describes the reditio completa ad se ipsum of the mind.

4. Sense Knowledge. From the fundamental law that knowledge is always and necessarily knowledge of self, we can deduce the metaphysical structure of an object known through the senses. The sensing being has involved his own self in the selfness of the other, so that inasmuch as it exists as a knowing being it is the other. The other must however be understood as the substantial other; the relative identity

of the sentient being with the other is an identity in non-identity. Otherwise the sentient being would have his own self as his first knowledge. This other, itself a substance, is accidentally identical with the sensible knower. From this it follows that both must have the same structure. If they were different, no kind of identity could be realized. The first-known other of the sensible knower, the *objectum proprium* of the sensibility, is therefore like the latter, a material being, that is, an existent whose being has been communicated through its otherness to pure otherness. It is composed of matter and form. Should we change our point of view however and consider the cognitive process in which we start from material beings, which are the objects of the sensibility, we would then be describing the process of abstraction, the *reditio completa ad se ipsum*.

The material being is metaphysically composed of form and matter. Because its essence is so composed, its activity is also material. For activity is the *actus secundus* of essence; the essence expresses itself in activity. If man in his sensibility brings to completion the activity of an object, he brings into being an *exemplatum* of the essence of this object. When this accomplishment of the activity in the sensibility is completed, it will also be conscious; man knows the object by his senses, indeed not in its essence, but in its completed activity.

How is it possible however for a material being to reach its fulfillment in the sensibility which is the term of its activity? The effect must belong to the same level of being as the cause. Since the cause is material in this case, how can it influence the sensibility which, as a faculty of cognition, is higher in the realm of being? For the sensibility as cognitive "hovers midway" between a total immersion in the exteriority of matter and an intrinsic ontological independence with respect to it: consequently, the act of sensation is in undivided unity with the material (actus materiae) and, as such, material, yet is also an act of assertion of being (forma) over against matter (actus contra materiam).[34]

The traditional solution is simple; the material being acts upon the material corporeity of the sensibility. Since the sensible faculty is intrinsically dependent on matter (here the concrete matter is meant), it is therefore also in its essence intrinsically dependent on it. If this concrete matter now were to change in its essence, the sensibility also must change in a way proportionate to the change that took place in the matter. If the material being influences the purely material foundation of the sensibility, and appears as actio, then this actio will be brought to completion by the sensibility. This faculty, since it is intrinsically dependent on concrete matter, takes possession of this actio and completes it in accord with its own capacity. This completion of the material being in the medium of the sensibility is therefore simultaneously effected actively by the sensibility, without this activity being different from the pure reception of the determination: actio est actus agentis et patientis.[35]

St. Thomas calls this completion of the material being in the medium of the sensibility the species sensibilis. The species therefore is not an image or double of the external object, but its completion. The species as self-completion of

[34] K. Rahner, Geist in Welt, 93–94.
[35] K. Rahner, Geist in Welt, 95–109.

the *res sensibilis* through the medium of the sensibility belongs to the being of the object itself, because every effect
of an *agens* is a *perfectio agentis*. On the other hand this
self-completion of the material being can unfold and exist
only in the sensibility as its medium: on that account the
species can enjoy conscious possession of itself and so be
known only in the sensibility.

For our purpose, it is not necessary that we treat here of
the apriority of space and time, of the *memoria*, *phantasia*
and *vis aestimativa*.[36] The next question, the passage of the
species sensibilis from the *phantasma* to the *species intelligibilis*, is much more important for the development of
our thought. So we will proceed now more in detail and
take pains to remain close to the terminology of classic
scholasticism.

5. *"Phantasma"* and *"Intellectus Agens."* How can this
phantasm bring forth a *species intelligibilis*, an act of intellectual knowledge? How can the phantasm that is in itself
immaterial to be sure, but yet intrinsically dependent on
matter, be the cause of a *species* which, since it is intellectual, is intrinsically independent of matter? How can a
cause bring about an effect which is more perfect in the order of being than the cause itself?

The scholastics answer that the proper cause of the
species intelligibilis is not the phantasm, but rather the
man himself through his *intellectus agens*. The phantasm
does not cause the intellectual cognition; this would be a
mechanistic-materialistic point of view. Cognition is an
actio immanens, self-completion of the being. The *species*

[36] G. Siewerth, *Die Apriorität*, 135–167; K. Rahner, *Geist in
Welt*, 304–311.

intelligibilis, as the constitutive element of cognition, must therefore primarily be brought to fulfillment by the man himself: the phantasm is related to it as an instrumental cause.

We have already seen that the phantasm, the *species sensibilis*, although it is "taken" from external objects, is not a pure passive determination of the sensibility. It is much more the self-completion of the sensibility because and insofar as it is itself caused by the sensibility itself. We have also seen that, according to St. Thomas, the understanding is the source of the sensibility. The sense faculty has its origin in the understanding and is ordered toward it. This relation of origin is essential to a proper understanding not only of the process but also of the inner structure of the understanding and the sensibility.

If the sensibility attains its goal when it produces the phantasm and *species sensibilis*, then this is due to the activity of the understanding as the source of the sensibility. The phantasm is therefore produced through the understanding itself, since the understanding has embodied itself in matter as sensibility. Here lies a counterpart to the relation which we call *anima ut forma corporis*. The soul, as *forma corporis*, is the act of the body; it is body and yet, as intellectual soul, reality in itself; in this sense it is not body, but rather possesses a body. Thomas formulated it this way: *forma quae est per se subsistens habet aliquem modum inquantum est res quaedam subsistens, et quendam modum secundum quod est actus talis subjecti.*[37] If we apply this to the understanding and to the phantasm, we must then say: the understanding as an intellectual act (intrinsically inde-

[37] *In IV Sent.*, d. 49, q. 2, a. 3 ad 3

pendent of matter) possesses one mode of existence; it possesses another mode of existence insofar as it is intrinsically dependent on matter (no longer as understanding, but as sensibility). Therefore we can in this sense say that the understanding produces the *species sensibilis*. In this sense we affirm that the phantasm is always in the medium of intellectual cognition.

The understanding, without completely losing its spirituality, has passed over into the sensibility. Thus, in the sensibility, the understanding "is" sensibility in the same way in which the soul "is" the body. Since however the understanding has not become completely corporeal as sensibility, but remains an intellectual form, it can lay hold of the phantasm and take it into itself. Scholastics call the understanding, insofar as it is united to sensibility, *intellectus agens*; the understanding, insofar as it takes up the phantasm as *species intelligibilis*, they call *intellectus possibilis*. The gap therefore that exists between the understanding and the sensibility is bridged over by the inner dynamism of the understanding itself.[38]

6. *Abstraction and "Conversio ad Phantasma."* It has already been shown that the *species sensibilis* is the second act of a form which belongs to the reality of the object. It was also indicated that this form, although it is grasped and influenced by the sensibility, has been detached so far from matter that it now is just as immaterial as the sensibility itself. It already exhibits here, in sense knowledge, a certain "abstraction"; this form, which in origin was a material form, became through the medium of the sensibility a form that is immaterial in itself, although it remains still in-

[38] K. Rahner, *Geist in Welt*, 236–242

trinsically dependent on matter. This detachment from matter, this abstraction, is the reason why this form becomes a form of knowledge; it is nevertheless not the same as that which the scholastics commonly designate as abstraction.

Abstraction in the scholastic sense is first exhibited when the phantasm is received by the understanding as *species intelligibilis*. Because the phantasm is grasped by the understanding and comes to completion through the medium of spiritual immateriality, it becomes as immaterial as the intellect itself; from the sensible phantasm that intrinsically depends on matter, there arises an intellectual *species* that is intrinsically independent of matter.

But what is immateriality? It is a negative term, and as such is not helpful. To understand the *species intelligibilis* in its structure, we must strive for a positive knowledge of that which is negatively designated as immateriality.

Immateriality is the negation of matter. Matter is introduced as the intrinsic condition of possibility for the fact that a being is not cognitive. Immateriality signifies therefore nothing else than being that is present to itself, that is, spirit. If we want to define positively what *species intelligibilis* is, we must try to grasp it as an essential form in the medium of the human spirit. What happens when a phantasm becomes a form which, determining the human spirit, is brought to completion by it? What is the human spirit?

Being signifies absoluteness, and so, also, unlimitedness. Existence then, insofar as it is Being, is likewise absolute and unlimited; through essence it is relative and limited. Since existence is endowed with greater ontological power than This new being, which passes beyond limits of essence to complete itself through a new perfection, its activity.

This new being, which passes beyond limits of essence to exist as accident, is the actuality of the human spirit (*actus secundus*).

The spirit must be in some way absolute and unlimited; if it had no absoluteness and unlimitedness, it would have no Being. If it had no Being, it could not exist in second act. Yet if the mind were simply absolute and unlimited, it could not exisit as second act of a finite agent, but could only exist as Absolute Being. Since the mind must on the one hand be in some way absolute and unlimited, and on the other hand cannot be made identical with Absolute Being, it can only exist as something that is necessarily directed toward the Absolute Being and determined by it. For that which is directed to the Absolute is in itself relative and yet absolute and unlimited; it is relative, because it is not the Absolute Being; it remains absolute, because that which is necessarily directed to the Absolute is an absolute relation. The human spirit [*in actu secundo*—tr.] is accordingly a second act [of a finite being—tr.], an accident, that is directed to the absolute and is unlimited: Absolute Being is the horizon of the human spirit.

The unbounded horizon of the human spirit enters as the transcendental condition of possibility for a question about Being, indeed for any question. For any empirical question, that is, one which examines experience and seeks its answer in experience, cannot be raised as a subject of inquiry through previous knowledge which is purely empirical (otherwise the question would not even be possible), but has also as its condition of possibility a previous knowledge of Being which is metaphysical in character. When one asks: "What is that?" he knows that "that," namely the empirically present and known, reveals a further and deeper "what," something not yet present or known, which it actually and ultimately "is," yet which still remains to be inquired into. Therefore the question, just as the judgment, presupposes the unconditioned horizon and therefore the unlimited value of Being.[39]

If now the *species intelligibilis* is completed through the medium of the soul, it exists as immaterial, that is, it is placed in the unlimited horizon of Being. A form however that is placed in the horizon of Being is completed and known as a limited form; a singular against the background of Being. By the very fact that the form is known as a limited one, a field of unlimited possibilities is also made known at the same time. For the limits of something are only known as limits when man has grasped something beyond them. The form of the singular, as far as it is known in the possibility of its manifold repetition, is a universal form. This is the source of the knowledge of universals.[40]

The *species intelligibilis* therefore, through the medium of the soul, becomes an act of knowledge which embraces the universal and the concrete singular at the same time. The universal is known through the fact that the singular, which is seen against the horizon of Being as one of many possible beings, reaches its fulfillment as a partial element in the total universe of beings.[41]

The *species* is thus not merely a grasp of the universal; the fact that it proposes the singular as a limited thing is the condition of possibility for the knowledge of the uni-

[39] E. Coreth, *Metaphysik als Aufgabe*, 51.
[40] K. Rahner, *Geist in Welt*, 196–218.
[41] K. Rahner, *Geist in Welt*, 183–192.

versal in the singular. The spirit however is in possession of the *species* of the singular inasmuch as the former is related to the sensibility and informs the phantasm. St. Thomas calls this turning of the spirit to the sensibility the *conversio ad phantasm*; this *conversio* however is essentially one with the *abstractio*, which is considered the reflective movement of the soul. *Abstractio* and *conversio* are merely aspects of the one event. So from *abstractio* and *conversio* there arises the *species intelligibilis*, which mediates the universal in the concrete singular.[42]

There are different meanings attached to *species intelligibilis* by the scholastic philosophers, relative to our earlier discussion. Some assert that the *species intelligibilis*, inasmuch as it is brought into being by the understanding, is always abstract; in other words it is a universal representation. Others say that the *species intelligibilis* is concrete. In the first case, knowledge of the singular is explained through a *conversio ad phantasma* which occurs subsequently. In the second case, the genesis of the universal is explained by an activity of the understanding whose precise nature is left unspecified.[43]

Looked at phenomenologically, the situation is this: we know the universal and the singular at the same time, in one single intuition, which represents the object as concrete and abstract. Only subsequently can we uncover a universal aspect and observe it by itself. In this phenomenological evidence we find confirmation for our affirmation of the real identity of *conversio ad phantasma* and *abstractio*.

[42] K. Rahner, *Geist in Welt*, 271
[43] J. J. Urraburu, *Institutiones Philosophicae*, vol. 5: "Psychologiae pars secunda," Vallodolid/Paris/Rome 1896, 887–898.

Even looked at metaphysically, both theories appear to have their difficulties. For if we assert that we primarily know the universal, then the knowledge of the singular must be explained by a subsequent *conversio ad phantasma*. But the process of knowledge and also the knowledge of the universal is generally a *conversio ad phantasma*, an informing of the phantasm. And it is difficult to see how a subsequent *conversio* can produce something new, something that was not already present due to the primary *conversio*. The *species* is indeed always referred back to the phantasm; a subsequent *conversio* seems to be able to produce nothing new, nothing that was not already in the *species* from the beginning.

But if we say that the *species intelligibilis* is first of all simply knowledge of a singular, then we are presuming that a form can be placed against the horizon of being, without being already abstract by the very fact of its being placed against this horizon. The problem of the universal then becomes even more acute; indeed in our opinion it becomes insoluble. There is no need for us to go into the question in more detail however since, in this section of the book, we are drawing on the work already done by Karl Rahner. In his book, *Geist in Welt*, Rahner makes evident the real identity of *abstractio* and *conservio ad phantasma*; this is the leitmotif of his exposition.[44] But if the *abstractio* and the *conservio ad phantasma* are merely two aspects of a single process then we must maintain that the *species intelligibilis* is an act of knowledge which embraces the universal and the singular simultaneously. In this act of knowledge we find the borderline between the abstract and the individ-

[44] K. Rahner, *Geist in Welt*, 271.

ual, since it unites both in itself: in it we have knowledge of
the universal in the singular.

Our explanation of the *conversio ad phantasma* and of
the simultaneously abstract and concrete character of the
species intelligibilis, as we mentioned, is not held commonly
by scholastics. Many consider the abstraction and the *conversio* differently, but the common scholastic tradition is
united on this point, viz. that the *species intelligibilis*, described as the end product of the abstraction, can represent
both a universal and a singular. The *species* is therefore not
always concrete and not always abstract, but can be both.
We stress this here only because this slender basis can serve
as the starting point of our next consideration.

B.   The "Species Intelligibilis" as Intuition

The scholastic textbooks of metaphysical psychology treat
of abstraction in a chapter that is usually entitled "*Theoria
Abstractionis*" or "*De Origine Idearum.*" There they speak
of ontologism, traditionalism and innate ideas; the *solutio
scholastica seu doctrina de abstractione* appears in connection with the refutation of these systems.[45] In the following
chapter, which is often entitled "*De Conceptu, Judicio,
Ratiocinio,*"[46] they prove that the concept is a *verbum mentis*, that it is the *medium in quo res attingitur*, that the judgment presupposes the *simplex apprehensio*, and so forth.
When we read both of these chapters, we cannot help

[45] P. Siwek, *Psychologia Metaphysica*, Rome 1939, 268–284.

[46] P. Siwek, *Psychologia*, 284. The title: "de metaphysica struc-
tura actus intellectivi" (284) is quite characteristic. What is intended is the concept. The structure of the judgment is discussed
in a concluding section, "de judicio" (314 ff.)

thinking that something important remains unsaid. There is a break between these two chapters; it is as if the theory of abstraction has nothing to do with the following chapter. There is no real transition. After we have carefully inquired into the evolution of the *species intelligibilis*, after we have proved that the phantasm, through the activity of the *intellectus agens*, is received by the *intellectus possibilis*, and reaches its perfection as *species intelligibilis*, we naturally expect that there will be some explanation of the *species intelligibilis*. But there is none. Rather we get the impression that the inquiry into the nature of the concept, the judgment and reasoning is on an entirely different level than that of the *species intelligibilis*.

This break in the chain of thought, this lack of transition is of interest to us. We must begin here. May we ask: what connection does the *species intelligibilis*, shown to be the ultimate result of the abstraction, have with the concept, the judgment and the chain of reasoning? How are they joined with one another? Can we simply equate the *species intelligibilis* with the *conceptus?* Is the *species*, which was proven to be the ultimate result of the abstractive process, nothing other than the concept? Or is it a judgment? Or, perhaps, is it what the scholastics call the *simplex apprehensio?* And how is this *species* connected to what the neo-scholastic theory of cognition calls "evidence?" We must occupy ourselves with these questions which arise directly from both the formal treatment of abstraction and the development given to it in the scholastic textbooks.

Whether the concept is a *species intelligibilis*, or whether the judgment or the syllogism are one or more *species intelligibiles*, is not our question now. The concept, the judg-

ment, the syllogism, and evidence also, are acts of intellectual cognition. As such, they are *species intelligibiles* or a
complex of such *species*. The concept however is one *species
intelligibilis*, and the judgment another. There are many
species intelligibiles, diversified in their structure; they are
as different from each other as are the acts of knowledge
which correspond to them. Our question here is whether
that definite *species intelligibilis*, whose structure as the end
product of abstraction has been the subject of our investigation, is identical with the concept, the judgment, the *simplex apprehensio*, or with what is called evidence. This and
this alone is the question which concerns us now.

Since the syllogism is nothing but a definite succession
of judgments, we do not have to ask expressly whether the
species intelligibilis is the same as the syllogism. For if it is
shown that it is not the judgment, then we also know that
it cannot be a syllogism. It suffices therefore if we direct our
investigation to the other types of intellectual cognition.

1. *The "Species Intelligibilis" and the Judgment.* Since
the *species intelligibilis*, in the very specific sense we have
given to the term, cannot be a judgment, it follows that
there is no separation of subject, predicate and copula in
the *species*. The nature of the judgment is such that in it a
double synthesis takes place, the concretive synthesis and
the affirmative synthesis.[47] The judgment is a concretive
synthesis inasmuch as in it the predicate, which is a universal concept, is joined to the subject. It is a veritative synthesis, because the predicate is joined to the subject through
the copula "is"; in other words, the concretive synthesis is
established as an existing, or at least as an independent

[47] K. Rahner, *Geist in Welt*, 134–143.

"something" in a negative or affirmative sense. Through this veritative synthesis, the totality is placed in being; it is referred to reality, to the *noumenal*, so that this judgment is now true or false.

The *species intelligibilis* however does not exhibit these characteristics. Yet it is true that the *species* is always related to the sensibility, and through this to reality. In this sense we can say that a *species* must be true or false: for there must take place—or be absent—in it an *adaequatio intellectus ad rem*; this adequation, as a partial element of the *species*, is also known as much as the *species* itself. The *species* therefore is something that contains truth; indeed, *continet veritatem formalem*. But there is no question of a real synthesis here. For synthesis supposes that both the elements which are now united were previously separate from one another. But we cannot assert that a synthesis takes place in the *species* by means of which the *species* is related to the thing, to reality. For the *species* is always so referred by its whole essence. The most we can say is that such a veritative synthesis, when it is observed in the *species*, can only be called "synthesis" in an unreal sense.

The other essential element of a judgment however, the concretive synthesis, decides the issue. For it is in no way present in the *species*. There is no separation of subject and predicate in the *species*. Subject and predicate are posited as identical in the concretive synthesis, but this identity occurs in an act in which both are formulated as individual and therefore in some way not identical. It belongs to the nature of the judgment that subject and predicate are logically—that is, on the cognitive level—separated. The copula "is" refers to a real "thing" and thus affirms both as ontically realized in the same being. Nothing of all this takes place however in the *species intelligibilis*. The *species* has neither subject nor predicate; it is the single, undivided cognition of the external object. In it there is no distinction between subject and predicate; it is simply the spiritualized phantasm. And because no such concretive synthesis takes place in the *species intelligibilis*, it cannot be a real judgment.

Someone might object that there are also implicit judgments, in which subject and predicate are not separated. Could not the *species* be such a judgment? First, let it be said that implicit judgments, according to the thought of most scholastics, are secondary phenomena which, by their nature, are similar to the real, explicit judgment. The fact that the subject and predicate are not named singly still does not prove that there is no separation of subject and predicate. For if we say *"pluit,"* in this implicit judgment nothing different happens than when we say "it is raining." The English formulation of this content, which means the same as the Latin and clearly contains no different inner act, is not an implicit but an explicit judgment. Implicit and explicit judgments are only distinguished according to whether the logical, cognitive nonidentity of subject and predicate is grammatically expressed or not. The distinction therefore lies not in the structure of the judgment as a cognitive act, but rather in the formulation intrinsic to its spoken expression, in the structure therefore of the judgment insofar as it is expression [*Aus-sage*].

But if someone still asserts that there are implicit judgments which contain no concretive synthesis, and which therefore recognize no distinction between subject and predicate, then we must concede that there is such intellectual cognition. But the question is whether we can call this a "judgment." An implicit judgment, thus understood, is so essentially different from the real judgment that it is really not a judgment at all.

The *species* is an intellectual cognition which is aware of its own relation and adequation to the reality of the external object. If we take this *species* to be an implicit judgment, we are not incorrect in so doing. But it is then a question of terminology. We can call it an implicit judgment. But then we will always be trying to grasp the *species* as a simple abstract cognition; but it is not this, for it represents the thing not only as something abstract, but also as something concrete and individual. We would then always be in danger of regarding the *species* as a judgment, in such wise that it would not be very distinct from the explicit judgment; the *species* however is essentially, according to its structure, distinct from the real judgment. It is therefore better to avoid such ambiguous terminology. There is nothing which forces us to designate the *species* as an "implicit judgment" (in the above-mentioned sense). The expression "judgment" has a definite meaning: it denotes the concretive and veritative synthesis of concepts. Therefore we can say that the *species intelligibilis* is not a real judgment. We cannot decide yet whether, or in what way, it is connected with the judgment, but we shall return to this later.

Because the *species intelligibilis* is not a real judgment, because it is distinct from the judgment by its very nature, it is also not a syllogism. For a syllogism is merely a definite succession of judgments. And the *species* is not the latter.

2. *The "Species Intelligibilis" and the Concept.* Can

we equate the *species* with the concept? For the concept does not signify a concretive synthesis; it does not contain a distinction between subject and predicate; it has no copula.

Yet the *species intelligibilis* is not a concept. For the *species continet veritatem formalem.* It represents the object simultaneously (but from different points of view) as something universal and as something concrete and individual. Truth however is not in the concept. The concept is abstract and therefore does not represent the concrete as such. The concept is defined by the scholastics as *repraesentatio quidditatis intellectiva.*[48] Many neo-scholastics complete this definition by bringing the abstract character of the concept expressly into the definition. J. de Vries, for example, defines the concept as *repraesentatio intellectiva eaque abstractiva quidditatis.*[49] He does not develop a new thesis with this fuller expression of the definition. He relies on the scholastic tradition, which has always considered the concept an abstract type of cognition: that is, one which represents a whatness, but a whatness that is not related to a definite individual. Following the tradition, de Vries writes:

Indole sua "abstractiva" conceptus opponitur speciebus intellectualibus spiritus puri;[50] conceptus de se sunt universales; nimirum cum sint repraesentationes abstractivae, non praebent concretam et singularem rem secundum totam ejus plenitudinem, sed tantum notam quandam seu notas, quae sunt universales.[51]

---

[48] J. de Vries, *Logica cui praemittitur Introductio in Philosophiam,* Freiburg i. Br. 1952, nos. 151–157, 164–165.
[49] J. de Vries, *Logica,* no. 151
[50] *Ibid.*
[51] *Ibid.* no. 164

This definition, nevertheless, does not apply to the *species intelligibilis,* which we have shown to be the end product of the process of abstraction. For the *species* represents the concrete in its entire fullness; the totality is raised to the intellect's level of immateriality; the totality is known as *species.* The *species* represents the object as a universal, but also as something concrete. The *species* is merely the spiritualized phantasm. Thus we cannot say of the *species* that *non praebet concretam et singularem rem secundum totam ejus plenitudinem, sed tantum quandam notam,* for the *species,* because of the *conversio ad phantasma,* is always a cognition, which represents the concrete whole. And because the definition of the concept is not applicable to the *species,* we can affirm that the *species* is not a concept.

Moreover, the concept does not contain formal truth. It is not actively related to the *thing,* to the being as actual. As the scholastics express it, the concept possesses no *veritas formalis.* De Vries adds:

Conceptus ergo exhibet quid (vel quale) sit objectum quoddam, nondum autem de obiecto aliquid enuntiat;[52] *patet quod in simplici conceptu nondum "dicitur aliquod esse," sed tantum quidditas quaedam apprehenditur; nemo enim audito solo simplici vocabulo (v.g. "homo"), quod est signum conceptus, dicit aliquod verum vel falsum dictum esse, sed exspectat, qualis propositio (v.g. de homine) formetur.*[53]

The *species* does however contain formal truth. It is actively related to the being, to the actuality of the object. For this *species,* which is nothing other than the spiritualized phantasm, represents everything that the phantasm it-

[52] *Ibid.* no. 152
[53] J. de Vries, *Critica,* Freiburg i. Br. 1954, no. 30.

self has represented; it presents it in relation to the being itself. If I have a phantasm of this bookstand, and if, through
the activity of the *intellectus agens*, this phantasm is spiritualized as *species*, then this *species* represents the bookstand
as it is and not otherwise; it represents it as existing, actual
being. The *species* is referred directly to the object; it is
the bearer of truth. And therefore it cannot be equated with
the concept. They are essentially different from one another, because the essential elements of the concept are not
realized in the *species*.[54]

Can we not regard the *species* as a single concept, as a
conceptus singularis? The *conceptus singularis* "*hic homo*"
will not represent a universal but, on the contrary, since we
grasp the *hic* and the *homo* as a single totality, it represents a
concrete thing.

This concept also seems to contain formal truth, for it
affirms this man as existing; it is referred to the being itself.
This understanding of a *conceptus singularis*, which is not
in harmony with tradition (according to tradition, we
cannot treat the *hic* and the *homo* as a totality), is a problem
in itself. We can however say that a *conceptus singularis*
thus understood essentially coincides with what we call intuition. The advocates of such a *conceptus singularis* mean
thereby that which we shall describe as intuition. But
we must stress that it is not a real concept. The traditional definition of concept can no longer be applied to it.
Such a particular concept is really not a concept at all.
That is the reason why many authors designate the same
thing by the term "implicit judgment." What they are

[54] J. Siewek, *Psychologia*, 268–289

talking about is always the same: namely that cognition which is neither a real concept nor a judgment, and which comprehends the object simultaneously as abstract and concrete. What they are talking about is therefore the *species intelligibilis.* The designation however is unfortunate.

3. *The "Species Intelligibilis" and the "Simplex Apprehensio."* Simplex apprehensio has been used in different senses by the scholastics, especially in the earlier period. Since we cannot possibly go into the history of the development of the concept of *"simplex apprehensio,"* we shall take it to mean what most of the neo-scholastics understand by it. *Simplex apprehensio,* according to them, is the concept, insofar as it is understood as an act of the intellect. *Conceptus ut actus intellectus seu subjective spectatus . . . dici solet "simplex apprehensio." . . . Apprehensio simplex dicitur in oppositione ad "apprehensionem enuntiabilem"* (i.e. contentum judicii), quae est apprehensio composita.[55]

The *simplex apprehensio* is, accordingly, equivalent to the concept; it is the concept insofar as it is looked upon as act. Therefore it is already evident that the *species intelligibilis* cannot be the *simplex apprehensio.* We have already shown that the *species* is by its nature different from the concept. For if the *species* is by its nature essentially different from the concept, it cannot coincide as act with the concept, and accordingly with the *simplex apprehensio.* For the content of an intellectual cognition is the form of this cognition, insofar as it is an act. If the form of one intellectual cognition is essentially different from the form of another cognition, then these cognitive acts are essentially different.

[55] J. de Vries, *Logica,* no. 152.

4. *The "Species Intelligibilis" and Evidence.* Evidence
is defined in the neo-scholastic theory of cognition as *clara
rei intelligibilitas*.[56] This expression *"intelligibilitas"* does not
mean a simple potentiality. *Intelligibilitas* does not mean
here merely "capable of being understood," but rather "actually being understood." De Vries writes:

> . . . ad evidentiam non sufficit rem in genere esse intelligi-
> bilem, neque etiam eam pro homine in genere esse intelligi-
> bilem, sed ad eam requiritur ipsam rem clare se hic et nunc actu
> manifestare. Huic manifestationi rei ex parte intellectus neces-
> sario tamquam correlatum correspondet clara perceptio rei, quae
> saepe dicitur evidentia subiectiva, opposita evidentiae obiectivae
> seu evidentiae simpliciter dictae, quae est clara rei manifestatio.[57]

Objective evidence therefore is the object's "being brought
to consciousness"; subjective evidence is the conscious "see-
ing" of this thing or state of affairs.

Accordingly, evidence is not a simple concept. It is the
"self-revelation," the self-disclosure of an object. To have
evidence, it is necessary that the object be actually known;
from this one can conclude that evidence, according to its
nature, is not necessarily abstract knowledge. It is the self-
disclosure of an object, and thus knowledge that also represents a concrete individual. And because in itself it is not
abstract, it cannot merely be a concept. Furthermore it cannot merely be a concept because the object discloses itself
evidentially in its own peculiar way; the object shows itself
as being, that is, as positive possibility or as actual.

Moreover, evidence is knowledge which is aware of its
own conformity to reality: *continet veritatem formalem.*

[56] J. de Vries, *Critica*, no. 136.
[57] *Ibid.*

For it is knowledge that is viewed as *criterium sufficiens* of truth: *veritas non tantum evidentia immediata sed etiam evidentia mediata certificari potest.*[58] De Vries in his theory of cognition writes: *Evidentia in eo est, quod id est clare se manifestat; ergo exprimendo id, quod evidens est, dico esse quod est,* i.e. *vere iudico.*[59] Now, since evidence is knowledge, it cannot serve as criterion for truth, indeed, as the ultimate criterion for truth, if it is not evident in itself. This means: if evidence is in itself evident, if it is conscious of its own truthfulness, then we need no other knowledge to convince ourselves of the truth of evidence. The concept is not referred to the being as a completed affirmation: *"non continet veritatem formalem."* And the judgment knows only of its own conformity to reality of its own truth, insofar as it relies on the corresponding evidence. Evidence however, this self-disclosure of the object, does itself contain formal truth and represents the object in its concreteness without a separation of subject and predicate; it is an intuition, knowledge of the concrete, of the individual.

Evidence is not only knowledge of the concrete and the individual, but also of the abstract, the universal. There is evidence of first principles, mathematical theorems, and so forth. There is also evidence which comprehends the universal as such.

Is this not the *species intelligibilis?* Evidence and the *species intelligibilis* have the same characteristics; they are, in contrast to the concept, not abstract, but primarily concrete knowledge, which is at the same time abstract: they

[58] *Ibid.* no. 134
[59] J. de Vries, *Critica,* no. 137

are conscious of their own truth (*continet veritatem formalem*); they are, in contrast to the judgment, a single view, in which there is no concretive synthesis. Therefore we can say that the *species intelligibilis*, described as the end product of abstraction, is identical with evidence. Because this structure of self-evident intuition belongs to both of these, and only to these two, they are identical. For in order that one act of knowledge be different from another, it is necessary that both exhibit different structures: their form must be essentially different. But this is not the case here. And yet evidence seems to be a broader concept than that of *species intelligibilis*. For evidence can be immediate evidence. The *species* however is always only a spiritualized phantasm; it has always an external source. We must therefore make our former assertion more precise and say that the *species intelligibilis* is evidence that we possess of objects which do not coincide with the activity of the understanding itself.[60] In this way we can positively determine what the *species intelligibilis* is.

The mere fact that we have been able to identify the *species intelligibilis* and evidence does not get us very far. For while the concept of evidence is used in neo-scholastic theories of knowledge, it does not appear in scholastic metaphysics. We must ask therefore how the *species* fits into the total structure of knowledge, how it is connected with the other types of knowledge. This will appear in the next section. First however we must compare the result of our

[60] The effect of this restriction is to place the emphasis in the development on the role played by the *species* as a medium of knowledge.

scholastic development with that which is commonly designated as intuition.

5. *The "Species Intelligibilis" as Intuition.*[60-a] In its daily usage, the concept "intuition" means a unique intellectual insight which unites many relationships into a single whole. It is applied first of all to artistic intuition, to the creative intuition, which grasps in the one concrete act many relationships, without any discursive medium. Such an intuition opens unsuspected dimensions of reality which always were "known" in principle, but which now manifest themselves for the first time in their full extent. Intuition signifies the intellectual view through which one sees the concrete object at the same time as both individual and universal, insofar as it is itself and also insofar as it points to a manifold of interrelationships.

When in daily speech we say: "I have an idea," we mean an intuition. This expression, which appears in English, French, Italian, Portuguese, Spanish, German and other languages, can mean many things. Yet all these meanings can be referred back to a single fundamental schema.

The writer says: "I have an idea" and means that original, rich, concrete and yet abstract knowledge which he will de-

[60a] The same interpretation which we propose can be found in the works of a number of neo-scholastic philosophers. I am indebted for this information to Professor Rüppel, a Brazilian scholar, who brought this fact to my attention. See F. Sladeczek, "Die intellektuelle Erfassung der sinnfalligen Einzeldinge nach der Lehre des heiligen Thomas von Aquin," *Scholastik* I, 1926, 184–215. B. Lonergan, "The Concept of *Verbum* in the Writings of St. Thomas Aquinas, IV. *Verbum* and Abstraction," *Theological Studies* 10, 1949, 3–40. J. de Vries, *Critica*, nos. 56, 66, 191. See also J. Santeler, *Intuition und Wahrheitserkenntnis*, Innsbruck 1934

velop and explicitate, and from which a novel will arise. The
businessman says: "I've got it" and means a knowledge not
yet analyzed, a knowledge which brightens up his prospects.
The philosopher says: "I have an idea" and means by it a
germ, not yet conceptual and scientific, a germ from which
he will construct a scientific theory. Even the mathematician in ancient times probably said: "I have an idea" when
he discovered the first axiom of geometry (as he contemplated the lines of a triangle which he drew in the sand).

In these cases, the foundation is the same; it concerns the
nonconceptual knowledge of a totality, in which the universal shines forth through the medium of the concrete individual. This knowledge is essentially nonconceptual: it
contains neither subject nor predicate. Therefore it is not a
real judgment, not a syllogism. It is not discursive; it is a
simple undivided insight, which grasps the totality as such.
This knowledge is at the same time concrete and abstract.
Depending on the individual case, either the universal or
the individual can occupy the foreground, and this to such
an extent that the other is almost lost to sight in the background. Yet both are there. And normally, both are known
in some way. The mathematician who observes the concrete triangle drawn in the sand and thereby discovers the
first axiom of geometry sees the universal through the
medium of the concrete individual. And the philosopher,
who builds a scientific, conceptual system from a simple act
of nonconceptual knowledge, sees also, at least in the background, that "something" which he will explain by means
of his philosophical system.

Ordinary, common use of speech has many phrases for
what is meant by "I have an idea," "I received a light," "I

finally see it," "Now I have it." But all these phrases mean the same thing as that which we usually call "idea," "vision," "insight," and denote as intuition.

Therefore if we assert that the *species intelligibilis* is an intuition, we are using this expression in the same sense that it possesses in common everyday usage. By intuition then we understand that "idea," "vision" or "insight," that act therefore which, without concept, judgment or discursive reasoning is the means of the knower's contact with a totality as such, a totality in which the universal shines forth through the medium of the concrete individual.

By intuition we do not mean knowledge of a concrete object which is entirely exhaustive; as we understand it, intuition is much richer than the concept, yet it is not exhaustive knowledge. By intuition we do not mean knowledge that is directly intellectual, that is, a knowledge which grasps a material object intellectually without the mediation of the senses. In this sense, no intuition is possible for man. By intuition we simply mean what the man who has not studied philosophy means when he "has an idea": that knowledge of a totality, which represents simply and nonconceptually the universal and the concrete, the universal through the medium of the concrete.

The *species intelligibilis* is such an intuition, because the *species* presents the existent as concrete and as universal: because it lets the universal shine forth in the medium of the concrete individual, because the *species* presents the existent as something which has actuality, because the *species* manifests the total structure of the being as a universal in a concrete.

The *species* is the spiritualized phantasm, which contains

everything which the external and internal senses received from the object. The sensibility receives the object as existing, and existing in a definite manner. These metaphysical structures are known not by the sensibility as such, yet they are nevertheless ontically contained in it. Now when this phantasm becomes spiritualized, when it becomes the species intelligibilis, all these structures become spiritual, present to themselves, and therefore also known in some way (objectively or nonobjectively, with greater or lesser clarity, depending on the term of the knower's attention). And with this fundamental structure of a being, Being itself is known in its metaphysical conditions. This cosmic knowledge comes to pass however in our grasp of a concrete singular as its medium: the universal shines forth through the medium of the individual.

One can well ask why it is that this insight into the complexus of Being, this "vision of the totality," remains in most cases below the level of conscious knowledge. I have a phantasm from many objects; this phantasm is then spiritualized and becomes the species. Yet these numerous species manifest to me simply the objects of everyday occurrence, objects that have no connection with metaphysics or with Being as a totality. According to what has been said here, every spiritualized phantasm, every species, would have to be a metaphysical insight. Yet this is not the case. We can answer this objection in the following manner. These manifold interrelationships, these metaphysical structures, are always contained in the species and are thus always known in some way. But they are not always known objectively. Our attention is not directed to them, and we overlook them in the same way as does the man who fails to see the individual trees because he is looking at the forest as a whole. A somewhat similar situation is found when an artist and a peasant look at the same picture by Rembrandt: both "see" the same picture, and still they see different pictures. The relation of the knower to the *species* is similar. According to the direction, the degree and the depth of the attention which he gives to it, he sees either trivialities or the most profound relations in the world of being.

We call the *species intelligibilis* intuition because this expression in its everyday usage means all that the *species* is, in contrast to the concept, the judgment, the syllogism, the simple nonconceptual knowledge of a concrete-abstract totality.

C. INTUITIVE AND ABSTRACT-DISCURSIVE COGNITION

We have seen that the *species intelligibilis*, the intuition, according to its essential structure, is different from the concept, the judgment and the syllogism. We must now ask: what connection does this have with conceptual and discursive cognition? It has already been shown that the intuition appears in the judgment as evidence; we must now develop this connection further. We should like to do it by synthesis, by briefly characterizing the individual phases of the process of cognition. We rely therefore on the results of the previous section as well as on phenomenological data.

1. *Intuition.* Through the activity of the understanding, which remains spiritual in sensibility, the phantasm is elevated with all that it is, and is placed against the un-

limited horizon of Being. Now since the spirit's dynamism overleaps the single phantasm and grasps together with it the horizon of Being, the individual form is comprehended as a limited one; by transcending limits this form is grasped in its limitation. However, to know a form in its limitation is to grasp it as "something broader"; it is not merely capable of being related to this concrete individual, but also to others, that is, it is fundamentally repeatable.[61] Nevertheless, this form is still grasped with all its transcendental relationships; it comes to completion as something which has been placed in the realm of Being.

The object is not merely known as a universal which shines forth in the concrete singular. In it, one knows also what an existent is and what Being really means. In this universal there appears an entire metaphysic; the object is grasped as an element of Being in its totality. This metaphysical structure which is contained ontologically in the species must also be grasped in some way or other. For nothing which reaches its perfection as a form in the spirit remains unknown. However this still does not mean that we always grasp it objectively, since to do that we must in addition direct our attention to it.[62] These metaphysical structures are given, of course, in every species; they have therefore become self-evident. No further attention is paid to them; we do not even "see" them anymore. If a person wants to engage in metaphysics, he must direct his entire attention to them; such a man will at length see what every-

[61] K. Rahner, Geist in Welt, 331–383.
[62] See Thomas von Aquin, In I Sent., d. 3, 2. 4, a. 5c.: "exigitur intentio cognoscentis."

one sees, and he will say what everyone has already known.

Species however mediates a universal, insofar as it is known as a limited singular. It is only in the concrete singular that the universal appears, for the concrete is the medium in which the knowledge of limit and its transcendence on the intellectual level takes place.

By reflection (*reditio*) it represents the object as a universal, in another reflection the same object is represented as an individual being. The universal is known in the concrete singular, metaphysical principles are seen in a single indivisible grasp of the concrete. *Species* is an intuition which is really distant from conceptual and discursive knowledge.

2. *Intuition and Concept.* When, from the content of the intuition, the understanding brings a universal aspect into relief, in a separate act, this is a concept. A concept is a universal aspect which is brought into relief, which is abstracted, and being thus separated, is contemplated. This concept is now "abstract," that is, it represents a universal, which can really exist in many situations. It does not include existence, nor does it indicate whether anything exists or not. It is not actually related to an existing being; to be sure, the contents of a concept can be realized *de facto* in many beings, but the concept itself does not indicate whether this is actually the case or not. For this reason a concept can be neither true nor false; it does not contain formal truth.

Since a concept arises from the intuition, since it is a universal aspect detached from the intuition, it follows that the intuition, the *species*, can be the sole origin of the concept. For judgment and syllogism presuppose concepts. And since we possess no innate concepts, and since concepts come from "outside," we must say that they originate in the intuition. And if someone wishes to assert that concepts do not originate in the intuition, but rather in another spiritual act of cognition, then he must adduce proof for this. In our opinion such a claim could never be established. For this reason and by virtue of the principle that "beings should not be multiplied without reason," we can say that concepts originate in the intuition. Thus we explain the nature of a concept from the structure of the intuition. In this way we have been faithful to the phenomena. For phenomena show us that we do not immediately abstract fully formal and changeless concepts from sensation. The formation of concepts is a laborious process: "the straining after concepts"; it is an analysis of a situation which man sees as a totality. Concepts come into being slowly; we must search for the conceptual formulization. We must scrutinize our concepts and strike this or that note out of their content. Often we must change a concept to include new notes, and so forth. All these phenomena remain inexplicable if we assume that concepts are abstracted directly from sensation, the sensible phantasm, through a natural, necessary and unconscious process.

Therefore there are two "abstractions," each fundamentally distinct from the other. Abstraction is the spiritualization of the phantasm, the process in which from the phantasm, the *species intelligibilis* or the intuition arises. But abstraction also is the analysis of the intuition, by virtue of which the universal concept exists. Both the foregoing are fundamentally distinct from each other despite their similar names.

Now we are able to make the nature of the "singular" concept comprehensible. The singular concept "this man" is nothing other than the universal concept "man" related to the intuition by the "this." In this way the universal concept is related to an individual being, to a singular concept. We know that this explanation is correct from the fact that by adding notes to a universal concept we can never construct a singular concept. For these additional notes are again universal aspects, and by a mere summation of universals we can never arrive at the singular. But this shows that the "this" ought not to be regarded as a universal aspect; it must be understood rather as a relationship. This relationship, which however ultimately refers to the individual being, must refer to it through sense knowledge, through the phantasm. This is the way of human knowledge. But if knowledge must come through the senses, then it must also come through the intuition, through the *species*, for this is the place where understanding and sensibility meet, this is the bridge which leads through the "phantasm" to the material being.

3. *Intuition and Judgment.* If the knower binds two concepts together (concretive synthesis) and posits them in reality (veritative synthesis), he is making a judgment. But the intuition which enters here as "evidence" is the criterion of the truth of the judgment. Evidence is the reason why a person judges this way and not that.

If one should form the judgment, say, "Peter is a rational animal," this is what happens. Sense knowledge, which must work together with all the intellect's activity, supplies the phantasm of Peter which then becomes the intuition "Peter" through the activity of the agent intellect. In this intuition everything is contained in a single unity. The understanding in its analysis draws the universal aspect "man" and also "animal" and "rational" out of the intuition. These concepts, then existing, are now bound together in a concretive synthesis: "This man is a rational animal." This totality is now related to being-in-itself (veritative synthesis). The knower can do this, that is, he can accomplish the concretive and veritative synthesis, because he sees in the intuition that these belong together, and because he sees in the intuition that "this man Peter" and "rational animal" are a concrete unity. The knower sees in the intuition that the state of facts expressed in the judgment is true.

The same holds for the syllogism or ratiocination. The data which we analyze with careful logic through a multitude of judgments is always already contained as a unity in the intuition. Accordingly, the intuition is the point of departure for all discursive thought. At the outset there is the undivided unity. Only when the intellect begins to analyze does there exist a multiplicity of concepts and judgments.

Therefore the intuition is, in respect to the judgment, precisely that which the neo-scholastic epistemologists call evidence. It is that first self-revelation of the object, the *intelligibilitas rei*.

4. *Intuition and System.* But intuition is more. It is also the ultimate goal of discursive thought. The analyzing intellect divides, separates, distinguishes in order to bring everything together again in a single synthesis. Conceptual discursive thought is therefore teleologically ordered to pass beyond itself and to transform itself once more into a single undivided intuition. Accordingly, the intuition does not

exist only at the outset, but also at the end of discursive thought.

In this connection perhaps it is best if we simply let St. Thomas speak. St. Thomas has presented this position with unmistakable clarity. He asks whether the *scientia divina* (that is, metaphysics) consists of intuition or of discursive thought:

> Ad tertiam quaestionem dicendum, quod sicut rationabiliter procedere attribuitur naturali philosophiae, quia in ipsa observatur maxime modus rationis; ita intellectualiter procedere attribuitur divinae scientiae, eo quod in ipsa observatur maxime modus intellectus. Differt autem ratio ab intellectu sicut multitudo ab unitate. . . . Est enim proprium rationis circa multa diffundi, et ex eis unam simplicem cognitionem colligere. . . . Intellectus e converso per prius unam et simplicem veritatem considerat, et in illa totius multitudinis cognitionem capit. . . . Sic igitur patet quod rationalis consideratio est principium rationalis secundum viam resolutionis, in quantum ex multis ratio colligit unam et simplicem veritatem; et rursum intellectualis consideratio est principium rationalis secundum viam compositionis et inventionis, in quantum intellectus in uno multa comprehendit. . . . Unde patet quod sua [that is, the *scientia divina*'s] consideratio est maxime intellectualis.[63]

St. Thomas here distinguishes *intellectus* and *ratio*. *Intellectus* is that simple undivided knowledge of a single *veritas*, in which, however, there is revealed a content full of individual objects of knowledge: *unam et simplicem veritatem considerat, et in illa totius multitudinis cognitionem capit*. *Ratio*, on the other hand, extends itself to many things: *circa multa diffundi*. *Intellectus* however, that simple undi-

[63] *In Boet. de Trin.* q. 6, a. 1c

vided knowledge which embraces plurality in unity, is the point of departure of *ratio*. Originating from *intellectus*, *ratio* extends itself over many objects: it divides, analyzes, distinguishes. Accordingly, *ratio* leads back to the *intellectus* as to its goal. The plurality which in the discursive analytical process is comprehended by *ratio* is bound together once more in a single unity, in a single vision: *colligit unam et simplicem veritatem*.

If we were to translate these words of St. Thomas into our technical language, they would read: intuition is the starting-point as well as the goal of discursive, conceptual thought. Intuition is that undivided simple kernel, that oneness in which many things are made manifest. Out of this intuition then arise by analysis (i.e. by division, distinction and separation) concepts, judgments and syllogisms. Conceptual knowledge is therefore nothing other than the unfolding of intuition. Thus a system, an intelligent structure of concepts and judgments, is a noble but always inadequate attempt to bring about the unfolding of unity into multiplicity. Conceptual discursive knowledge however is merely a stage in the complete evolution of our knowledge; it is not its final goal. Any system, be it ever so proud and mighty, can be no more than the penultimate stage of our intellect's unfolding evolution. The ultimate stage, the final goal, is once more intuition, the act of knowledge which embraces multiplicity in unity: *in uno multa comprehendit*.

If we now compare this doctrine of St. Thomas with phenomenology, we find that it is fully confirmed. Phenomenology shows us that intuition is in fact the beginning and end of discursive knowledge. Indeed, everyday speech bears witness to this. We say of a scientist who has thoroughly studied his field: "He has mastered his subject," "he has a commanding view of his subject." In these expressions, which evidently originate in the common mode of thinking and not in a preconceived philosophical system, the same meaning is always intended: such a man is said to be standing on a mountain and taking in an entire panorama in a single glance. This idea, transposed into a spiritual context, is exactly what we mean by intuition: one sees a multiplicity in a unity. Every philosopher who struggles to reach the truth is well aware from his own experience that his system is merely a poorer, fainter and less certain expression of that which he has grasped in a single intuition. He will probably have to say, with the great French thinker, that science is merely a circle in which one end meets the other.

Phenomenology leads us still further. For certainly it is not true that a particular intuition is the only point of departure and the only end point of discursive knowledge. Certainly this can be so. However, normally it is more often true that in the course of time many intuitions simultaneously accumulate around one single object. Then, from these many intuitions, conceptual discursive thought arises. At the end of the discursive process there are not many intuitions, but one single one which unites all the intuitions into one. When, for example, a school boy studies the geography and history of Europe in the first grade, he is constructing an intuition. But when in the course of his many further years of research he studies Europe again and again, can he be said to be forming new intuitions all the time, so that at the end of his academic studies he might have twenty different intuitions of Europe? No, the one original intuition is continually enriched by every new addition, without losing its proper unity. The "new" intuitions are integrated into the "old" intuition.

This is much more obvious in human relations. When I meet a man for the first time I form an intuition of him which, after the encounter, will be more or less conceptually analyzed. The more often I encounter this man and the better I come to know him, the richer and more meaningful this one single intuition becomes. In the course of time, this intuition becomes so full of meaning that I will no longer be able adequately to analyze it; I have come to know the man so well that I can no longer describe him to another. If I should try to do so, I would find out how poor, how inexact, how colorless a description would result.

Let us briefly summarize this section. A development of the inner dynamism of the scholastic problematic of the process of abstraction leads us to distinguish two distinct modes of knowledge: the intuitive mode and the conceptual discursive mode of knowledge. Intuition is that undivided simple glance which grasps many things in unity and contemplates the universal in the concrete. From the intuition comes the concept, which is nothing else than a universal aspect abstracted from the intuition. By synthesizing concepts (predicative and veritative syntheses) we form the judgment which gives expression to one state of facts grasped in the fullness of the intuition, whereas the intuition serves as evidence for the judgment. Intuition however is not merely the point of departure of discursive thought; it is its final goal as well. Our diverse individual acts of knowledge, concepts or judgments lose their individual existence in the course of time and are bound together once again in a single intuition.

2   Personal Knowledge

Not only abstract-discursive knowledge, but also intuitive knowledge, about which we spoke in the previous section, can at times have personal reality as its content. These types of knowledge however, considered from the point of view of their origin as acts, are not essentially personal. Personal knowledge, as we saw in our phenomenological description of it, is an act springing from the center of a person's being which, as an act of knowledge, either rejects or accepts a Thou in his personal character. This cannot be said however of either abstract-discursive knowledge or intuitive knowledge. Both are types of knowledge which deal objectively with "things," even when they have personal reality as their content. They do not spring from man's personal center; they are not attitudes of his total human personality. Neither do they involve acceptance or rejection of another; they are simply knowledge of what is given, of an object.

What then is personal knowledge? What is its a priori necessity? What is its essential metaphysical structure? With questions such as these we reach our central problem, the metaphysics of personal being. Taking as our point of departure the nature of the person and his personal freedom, we shall endeavor to arrive at a metaphysical understanding of the act of personal knowledge.

A. The Ego

1. *The Ego and the Other.* If I ask about the being of
the existent, I must know already what Being is. If I knew
nothing about being at all, then being would be, as far as I
was concerned, absolutely nothing; and a question about
absolutely nothing would be in reality the same thing as the
utter nonexistence of a question. Some prior knowledge
about being is therefore the transcendental condition of
possibility for my question about it. Since, through the placing of my question, being is present to itself in knowledge,
being and knowledge are seen therein to coincide. Their identity is thus established as the starting-point of my inquiry.

Still however I do not know what Being is; for if I knew
what Being is, then the answer would have forestalled the
question itself. The knowledge about being which is presupposed by my question is then seen to be a prior knowledge
which implies at the same time a lack of knowledge. This
lack of knowledge about Being, which like Being itself reveals itself as an ultimate and fundamental ground of possibility for my question, shows that I am not identical with
the Being of the existent. Lack of knowledge means lack
of identity. I have Being; but I am not Being itself. For if I
were identical with Being, then Being would have to have
been totally present to itself in my question. Were this the
case however, then ultimate and exhaustive knowledge of
Being would have been already possessed, and thus would
have made my question itself impossible.

Therefore the Ego is not Being. Yet Being is not simply

opposed to the Ego as the other. For the Ego "is"; and, to the extent that it "is," it participates in Being. The non-identity of Being and Ego are synthesized in a higher identity. Being belongs to the Ego and at the same time transcends it. This means, in the first place, that the Ego is limited in itself. It is determined not simply by Being, through which it is placed in the order of the real as a self-identical existent; it is determined also through essence through which it is constituted as an existent possessing this finite determination. For every existent which is not Being itself must be, since it is limited, this definite determined existent. Thus we have once more the composition in the finite being of existence and essence which was already mentioned earlier in our discussion.

This means furthermore that the Ego is already aware of its own limitation. If its finitude had not been given to it in every act of thought, then its knowledge would not have been knowledge of a finite determined object; it would have been the act of knowledge in which Being knows itself; and this means that the Ego would have to be Being itself. Since however the Ego knows its essence immediately, it experiences itself as a finite Ego which confronts Being in knowledge. In other words the Ego, insofar as it is composed of existence and essence, is not only inserted into the order of being, but into the order of knowledge also, as essentially finite.

The Ego however, which experiences itself as limited in the act in which it perfects itself through knowledge, has already transcended its limits by the very fact that it is aware of them. For we can become aware of a limit as such only when we transcend it. Knowledge of a limited reality means transcending its limits. Thus the finite Ego passes beyond its limitation by experiencing itself as limited, and in its knowledge touches, by anticipation, as it were, something which as non-Ego is the transcendental condition of possibility for its own limitation. And, in doing so, it already knows that this something lies beyond the limits of the Ego; it is the other.

The other is something which has Being, yet is not Being itself. For the Ego too is an existent. Being shows itself therefore as the higher Identity in which the nonidentity of the Ego and the other is included. Thus the other can be positively determined as an existent against the horizon of Being; i.e. it can be known as an existent which confronts the Ego in Being and in knowledge.

Since however the Ego requires the other as the transcendental condition of possibility for its own finite self-perfection through knowledge, the other is an existent. To put it more precisely: there must be at least one existent which confronts the Ego in being and knowledge as the other and in doing so makes the Ego possible.

Since in our discussion of sensibility and abstraction we presupposed that there are a multitude of existents, which exist as others, this same point can be expressed in scholastic terms as follows: the finite Ego, which is not Being itself, "can only know Being through its knowledge of a finite existent."[64] Therefore it can only know Being if it perfects itself through its knowledge either of itself or of the Other. The Ego can however be known as limited only if it tran-

----

[64] E. Coreth, *Metaphysik als Aufgabe*, 66.

scends itself and grasps the Other, as it were, in anticipation. Being is known therefore because the Ego knows itself and the Other in Being, which both possess yet which transcends them both.

2. *The Ego and the Thou.* We have already seen that the Ego is composed not only of essence and existence, but also of matter and form. The composition of essence and existence explains its finite determination: the composition of form and matter explains the "presence to others" which characterizes its knowledge and therefore its being also.

From this it immediately follows, in the first place, that the constitution of essence and existence and of matter and form in an existent is possible, that is, compatible with being. Since however the Other is an existent, it is possible then in principle that the Other too should be composed of essence and existence, matter and form.

In the second place, it follows that at least one existent which exists as Other is composed of existence and essence. If this were not the case, the Ego would not be able to experience its own limitation, and therefore would not know being through its knowledge of a finite existent, but would know it rather in itself. From what has already been said about the nature of sense knowledge, it likewise follows that there is an existent which confronts the Ego as a finite being. Furthermore we know that these existents, as objects of sense knowledge, are necessarily composed of matter and form. Consequently, there exisits an Other which is composed of essence and existence, and matter and form; and which confronts the Ego as a determined finite being.

An existent however that is composed of existence, form

and matter has a fundamental capacity to exist in a twofold manner. If the being, which is permeated by the otherness of matter and form, returns to identity with itself, then we have a *reditio completa ad se ipsum*. By this we mean an existent which is spiritually present to itself through its acts of knowledge and volition. Should being lose itself however in the pure otherness of matter, then we have an existent to whose essence spiritual knowledge and volition do not properly belong.

A more careful consideration of this distinction will enable us clearly to differentiate both of these possible modes of being. The existent whose being is lost in the pure otherness of matter with no return to self-identity is incapable of spiritual knowledge and volition, since intellection is a being's "presence-to-itself." This existent therefore is essentially neither with itself nor for itself. What cannot be with itself can never exist for itself, since reflection on the self is essentially beyond its possibilities. Being however demands to exist in itself and of itself and thus to be a perfection whose reality consists of being with and for itself. Such a material being therefore can only be with itself and for itself, if it is brought to its perfection in another being which itself is spiritual. This means however that only in the spiritual ego can nonspiritual reality be what it is of itself; only in the Ego does it reach its perfection. This implies the existence of a fundamental relation of subordination through which the nonspiritual existent is ordered to the Ego. The nonspiritual "is" for the Ego and "is" in the full sense only in the Ego.

The essential opposition of the nonspiritual and the Ego

reveals itself in a multiplicity of ways in the phenomenal world. The nonspiritual is a mere object ready at hand to be used for the perfection and enrichment of the Ego. The Ego takes it and calls it its own. It is related to the Ego as the useful, and finds its perfection and its meaning in the Ego which uses and shapes it. It is a mere thing.

Yet the Other can exist in another manner too. If its being is not lost in the otherness, but returns to self identity, the Other is in full possession of itself. It "is" not merely in itself but with itself and for itself. This means that it is a spirit, endowed with intellect and will. It has a meaning in itself since its self is really identical with itself.

This spiritual Other is open, as is the Ego, to the unlimited horizon of Being. For spirituality, presence-to-itself, means openness to the ultimate and the unconditioned which is Being itself. The spiritual Other possesses, exactly as does the Ego, the unlimited value of Being which is identical with itself. It can say "I am" just as Ego itself can. For the spiritual Other, which brings itself to perfection, brings it in the way in which spirit does, into contact with the knowledge and being which cannot be surpassed.

Thus the spiritual Other is manifested as the other Ego. It is an Ego which I am not myself, but which, as the Other, confronts my Ego in being and knowledge. This other Ego we call the Thou. Consequently, the Thou, like the Ego, is an existent which is composed of existence, matter and form, and which exists in, with and for itself. Expressed in scholastic terms it is *substantia individualis rationalis in se stans.*

This composition enables us to understand the essential

relation which the Ego and the Thou have to each other. They are related to one another as essentially equal realities in such wise that an essential subordination of one to the other is excluded. Relationships between Ego and Thou are therefore of an essentially different nature than those which exist between mere things.

B. The Personal Ego

1. *Volition.* Knowledge and volition were already previously defined in the discussion on the metaphysical background of abstraction. Knowledge is the bringing of the Ego to perfection in the Other insofar as it is the perfection of the Other as such. Volition, on the other hand, is the bringing of the Ego to perfection in the Other insofar as it is self-perfection. In knowledge the Ego becomes the Other; in volition the Ego posits the other precisely as self. In the one case, the Other confronts the Ego insofar as it appears in the identity of the process of perfection as that which still remains the Other. In the other case, in the very nonidentity of the Ego and the Other an identity is brought into being in such wise that the Other, although maintaining its own identity, reaches its perfection as my other Ego.

From this it is clear that in the Ego understanding and will are mutually included in each other. The will is "taken up into" [*aufgehoben*] the understanding as its perfection: *exercitium intellectus est appetitus quidam*. Likewise the understanding is "taken up into" [*aufgehoben*] the will as the content of thought which determines it: "*specificatio voluntatis est forma intellecta*." In other words, will and understanding are not merely correlative quantities; neither are they related to one another as merely external conditions. For the will is in the understanding in the measure in which it intrinsically constitutes it. It is the intrinsic, constitutive moment of the understanding itself. The same is true of the understanding in relation to the will. The *forma intellecta* as a content of thought which determines the will is simply not an external condition for the will's existence; it is an interior element of the will itself.

Does this mean however that understanding and will are merely different aspects of one and the same thing? Not at all. The expression "to take up into" [*aufheben*] is thus to be understood in its full sense. The will, to the extent that it exists as *appetitus* of the understanding, is no longer the will but the understanding. Its proper mode of being, that of will, is "taken up into" the being of the understanding. And the *forma intellecta* which determines the will as its content does not exist as understanding but as will.

The fundamental difference between understanding and will is thus preserved. Even more, the essential impossibility of deducing understanding from will or will from understanding has not been overcome. I cannot deduce the practical from the theoretical, nor the theoretical from the practical. This means that from the fact that there is a dynamism of the understanding, I cannot deduce the fact that there is a will which has the *forma intellecta* as a content of thought which determines it. If I should try to do this, such a "process of mediation" would bring me not to the will in the proper sense, but simply to the "volitional moment" of the understanding which, as its dynamism, is still the understanding itself.

The theoretical and the practical therefore condition one another, since they mutually constitute each other. One cannot be derived from the other then through a process of mediation. The old problem still remains with us therefore in all its acuteness. How can I metaphysically grasp the practical without making it a mere constitutive element of the theoretical? How can I understand the will insofar as it is precisely the will in distinction to the understanding?

It may well be asked if we are not therefore asking for the impossible here. Can we make the practical an object of our thought without making it *ipso facto* theoretical? Is not every metaphysics something theoretical in itself, so that even a "metaphysics of the practical" is in itself pure understanding? Must we not say that the will, insofar as it is grasped metaphysically, exists as a content of the understanding, and must therefore lose its own specific uniqueness? The gulf between the theoretical and the practical remains unbridged. What the will is in its ultimate uniqueness is something which I cannot know so long as I confine myself to what I know through thought alone; I can only know it through the experience of willing.

This does not mean that the practical is irrational, or that it is impossible to ground the specific identity of the will metaphysically. We can only refuse the challenge of the will to be grounded metaphysically if we are prepared to give up as unanswerable the question about the All; and this means giving up metaphysics itself. Thus *per exclusionem* one path alone remains possible. Since we cannot deduce the practical from the theoretical, we must show that the theoretical presupposes as its own transcendental condition of its possibility, a point where the theoretical and practical are one and the same. For if the origin of the theoretical and the practical is the same, then the theoretical is always the practical and vice versa. We must therefore find the place where understanding and will mutually constitute one another while still remaining understanding and will. This is the area of the personal.

The personal is the single source from which the theoretical and the practical spring immediately. It is the place in which the theoretical attains its perfection and in which the practical exists in its original fullness. The personal is an act in which understanding and will mutually constitute one another without losing their own specific character, that is, without passing over into the other. It is not an act of the understanding into which the will is taken up. Neither is it an act of the will in which the understanding exists as an essentially volitional reality. It must be an act which is constituted by understanding and will, but in which understanding exists as understanding and will exists as will.

This we must now attempt to show. And, if we succeed, all that we have said so far will take on a much deeper meaning, as we continue our discussion, using this fact as our central point of reference.

2. *Free Will* [*Volition*].   At the beginning of our metaphysical inquiry we found that the question concerning the Being of the existent was the transcendental condition of any question whatsoever. This question is not a mental structure of purely intellectual relations. It is not removed from space and time. The question of the starting point is an existential question. The place where it arises is the

center of concrete existence, living in space and time, as a vital quantity which is conscious of its own plenitude.

In this concrete question we discovered a number of necessary truths which have shown themselves to be the first mediating elements of metaphysics. From these truths we can deduce—at least in principle—a whole system of necessary metaphysical relations. We have explained a few of these ourselves; others were merely hinted at; and many others passed over in silence. Consequently, in every instance our thought has been developed within a framework of metaphysical necessity.

This necessity was derived from our existential inquiry into Being, so that all our previous insights together with their exigencies are grounded ultimately in the existential question. This question as a whole is not however necessary. I do not need at all, here and now, to ask about Being. I can raise the question at anytime—or choose to take a stroll instead. How then can I find the ground of necessity in a question which itself is not necessary at all?

We could attempt to avoid this problem by refusing to admit that the question is not necessary. There are those who claim that they can prove that the question in its concrete fullness is a necessary one, and that nothing can be found in it which is not necessary. Any proof of this sort is specious however, and presupposes what has to be proven; for in a system of pure necessity everything is necessary, since, if something were not necessary, its very lack of necessity would make it incapable of being understood at all. Although we cannot derive the non-necessary from the necessary through a process of mediation, this does not

mean that nothing contingent can exist. If then we refuse
to accept the non-necessity of the question of being, we
cannot justify our refusal on the ground that our starting
point is a system of pure necessity.

But (it may be objected on the other hand) necessity cannot be ultimately grounded in non-necessity. Therefore the
existential question in its concrete fullness is a necessary
one. Even here something is implicitly presupposed: viz.
that the necessity of a system whose origin is found in the
existential question must have its ultimate ground in that
question itself. We can admit without contradiction that
the necessity of the question is a hypothetical one: "Granted
that I ask, it follows necessarily . . ." It is not even necessary
that I ask the question existentially here and now. Necessity
would still, of course, be sought in thought; not in my existential thoughts however, the conditioned thought that I
am thinking here and now, but rather in an absolute
thought. Once I think, I enter the realm of necessity, and
my thought must take the form of necessity. That I should
emit this concrete act of thought does seem however not to
be necessary at all.

Is then the existential question a necessary one or is it
not? Taken as a whole it is not; for if it were, then there
would be nothing in it at all that was not necessary. It would
be absolutely necessary as a whole. But that which is absolutely necessary as a whole cannot be simply a question
about being; it must rather be Being itself, present to itself
in thought. For necessity means being, and absolute necessity means absolute being. The question which I ask about
being is however not absolute being; it is simply a question

which both possesses knowledge and lacks knowledge. This concrete act of asking then is necessary in its non-necessity. It is a whole that is necessary because it "is," and insofar as it "is"; yet it is a whole which as such is not necessary because it is not the absolute "is."

The existential question is necessary once it is asked, but that it should be asked is not necessary. This existential question however—something which is not necessary—must now in the process of our inquiry become the medium through which we arrive at its transcendental condition of possibility. The existential question arises from an act of position, an act from which can precede both the necessary and the non-necessary.

The act of position, in which both the necessary and the non-necessary have their origin, is an existent, since it is a real act of position, and therefore it is necessary. Its necessity is however a super-necessity in which necessity and non-necessity are so included that both can spring from it.

This act of position, furthermore, as an existent is always present to itself. It is therefore cognition. It reaches its perfection however not merely as cognition, but also as will. For it places in being not merely the Other, but also the Self. What is placed in being is indeed the Ego insofar as it asks about Being. This shows however that to place the Self in being is fundamentally possible. If however this act of position can place the Self in being, then it is will.

Knowledge and will are not however completely absorbed in this act of position. If knowledge were to absorb the will completely in this act of position, then only the Other as Other could arise in it; the Ego could not. If the will were to absorb the understanding, then only the Self could be placed in being; the Other could not. The act of position however, which is being conveyed as the transcendental condition of the non-necessity of questioning, places in being both understanding and will, both the Other and the Ego, both necessity and non-necessity.

This we call freedom. For it is personal being, that center of the Ego which bears in itself both understanding and will, and serves as the origin of both. As their fundamental ground, it places both necessity and non-necessity in Being. As the unity which places a multiplicity in being, it is the necessary condition for the question about Being which itself is necessary in the super-necessity which includes non-necessity.

Freedom is an existent and therefore also a perfection or an act. We call this act of freedom the free decision or personal attitude. This original act through which both intellect and will are placed in being against the horizon of being itself is implicitly contained in every other.

Thus it is now evident that understanding and will in the free act are essentially different from understanding and will insofar as they are not posited in freedom. Or more exactly, understanding insofar as it constitutes a free act of position is essentially different from understanding; it is something which itself is placed in being. In the one case understanding is a constitutive element of freedom; in the other case it is something placed in being by freedom, an external element of freedom. What this means is that personal being constitutes the innermost core of the Ego in which understanding and will reach their highest ontological perfection insofar as they constitute each other without absorbing each other. This is the *a priori* of personal being.

3. *The Rationality of Freedom.* Taking as our starting point the question *de rationabilitate electionis*, a subject of dispute among the scholastics, let us now attempt to bring to light the *a priori* of personal being. We shall show that what we have said about the essence of personal being is completely in accord with scholastic thought.

The freedom of will in scholastic psychology consists essentially in free choice. This is the real heart of freedom. For the "free" act of the will which follows the act of election is no longer free in itself (*non formaliter*), but is free only to the extent that it has proceeded from a free election (*virtualiter liber*).[65]

The free act of election is not an act of understanding, but rather an act of the will, an act of the *appetitus rationalis*. And yet the free choice has some connection with the understanding, since it is an act of the *appetitus RATIONALIS*. It is a reasonable choice; it comes into being in the light of knowledge. If the free choice is rational, then this can only be because a *judicium ultimo practicum*, an act of knowledge directed to action, precedes the free choice. This *judicium ultimo practicum* prior to free choice is an act of

[65] See Siwek: "Libertas voluntatis invenitur formaliter in electione, quae est 'ultima acceptio, qua aliquid accipitur ad prosequendum . . .' seu in activa determinatione. Quo fit, ut actus, qui electionem sequitur, non sit liber formaliter, sed tantum virtualiter, quatenus videl. electioni liberae originem suam debet. Electio ipsa est formaliter actus voluntatis (non rationis): 'nam quamtumcumque ratio unum alteri praefert, nondum est unum alteri praeacceptatum ad operandum, quousque voluntas inclinetur in unum magis quam in aliud' de Ver. 22, 15," *Psychologia*, no. 354.

the understanding, and it is *rationalis* in itself and of itself. If free choice follows this *judicium*, if it takes place in accordance with it, it is itself rational.

Here however we run into a serious difficulty. For it was said that the free choice is rational because and insofar as it follows a *judicium*, i.e. takes one for its own norm. But if this is so, is the free choice still free? If the free choice, in order to be a *rationabilis electio*, must be directed to a *judicium ultimo practicum*, then it is really no longer a free choice. For this *judicium* is not free; and if the free choice must be directed by it, it becomes itself a necessary and determined event.[66]

Our answer is that the free choice, despite the *judicium practicum*, is free, because this *judicium*, as an *ultimo practicum*, depends on the will. This act of knowledge ordered to action is an act of knowledge which is directed immediately to action because it is dependent on the will. That a *judicium practicum* becomes a *judicium ultimo practicum* is due to the operation of the will. If the free choice follows upon this judgment, then it is still free, since the

[66] "Electionem, utpote actum 'appetitus rationalis,' debet semper praecedere actus rationis. Si unquam voluntas ferret electionem sive praevio actu rationis, ferret eam caece atque adeo cessaret esse 'appetitus rationalis.' Ex quo fluit voluntatem non posse unquam ferre electionem contrariam ultimo judicio practico. Ferendo enim electionem contrariam ultimo judicio, ferret eam exclusive proprio suo Marte, i.e. sine lumine intellectus praelucentis, proindeque cessaret esse 'appetitus rationalis.'

"At hic statim exsurgit difficultas. Si electio sequitur infallibiliter judicium rationis, judicum autem rationis evidentia objectiva regitur, hinc necessitati subjacet, quomob electio poterit dici 'libera'?" P. Siwek, *Psychologia*, nos. 354, 355.

judicium ultimo practicum as such has as its cause the will.[67]

This means however that the will is the cause of this *judicium* precisely insofar as it is *ultimum*. This causal act of the will however is either free or it is not. If it is free, then this free act reaches its term as free choice; and, as free choice, it presupposes another *judicium ultimo practicum* prior to itself. This other *judicium ultimo practicum* would in turn depend on a free choice, which for its own turn would presuppose still another *judicium ultimo practicum*, and so on. If this causal act of the will is not free in itself, then the *judicium ultimo practicum* is dependent on something necessary and, as such, is no longer free. Since it is no longer free, the "free choice" following it is in turn no longer free.[68]

We can attempt to avoid this difficulty in somewhat the following manner. The free choice presupposes a *judicium ultimo practicum*. This is the form (*species*) which specifies the free act of the will. Because the free act of the will is determined by a cognitive *species*, it is also *rationalis*. Nevertheless its freedom is not impaired by this. There is in it no determinism produced in it by knowledge. For this

[67] "Quia hoc judicium pendet a voluntate; pendet autem ab ea non hoc sensu act si ipsa voluntas eliceretur—ut per se patet—sed quia ipsa efficit, ut hoc judicium sit ultimum." P. Siwek, *Psychologia*, no. 355.

[68] "Dices quomodo voluntas potest ut judicium rationis sit ultimum? Nonne ad hunc finem opus esset, ut voluntas imprimat intellectui positivam aliquam motionem? Sed si ita est, ulterius quaeri potest: praeceditne hanc motionem iterum aliud judicium instaurabis, ut patet. Si autem negative, tunc neque ad electionem faciendam opus erat judicio practico praevio." P. Siwek, *Psychologia*, no. 355.

judicium ultimo practicum is, to be sure, the essential determination of the free act of the will, but precisely as *ultimo practicum* it is dependent on the free act of the will. It is not dependent however on a free act of the will prior to itself—that would lead to a *processus in infinitum*—but simply on the act of the will which it specifies. In a flowing series of *judicia practica* we suddenly find an intervention by the will, and only that particular *judicium* fastened on by that intervention becomes an *ultimum practicum*.[69]

[69] "Resp.: Voluntas efficit hoc non per aliquem actum specialem a se elicitum et in intellectu receptum (motionem), sed quia immediate post aliquod judicium rationis actum 'electionis,' non exspectando ulterius 'ullum aliud judicium rationis.'

Quae ut bene capias, sedulo animadverte ad ea, quae sequuntur: a) electio nec praecedit judicium rationis nec ab eo praeceditur (tempore!), b) electio accipit specificationem suam a ratione, videl, ab illa forma intentionali, quae in judicio practico exhibetur. At bene adnimadverte, specificationem hanc non esse intelligendam eodem modo, quo specificatio intellectus possibilis (quae, ut notum est, fit per speciem impressam); voluntas enim non est facultas representativa objecti. Intelligenda est modo analogico: actus voluntatis dici tur 'specificari,' quatenus homo, qui vult (non voluntas, sed homo per voluntatem!), habet simul speciem intellectivam in se praesentem; c) quod attinet exercitium (seu in ordine efficientiae) electio pendet non a ratione sed a sola voluntate. Immo ipsum judicium practicum pendet in hoc ordine (i.e. quoad exercitium) a voluntate . . .

Quae cum ita sint, patet inter intellectum et voluntatem adesse dependentiam mutuam, causalitatem reciprocam: voluntas pendet ab intellectu in ordine causalitatis finalis, intellectus autem pendet ab voluntate in ordine causalitatis efficientis (Unde etiam praeacceptatio, qua voluntas judicium aliquid facit "ultimum" minime requirit actionem positivam in istud judicium exercitam). Non obstante hac causalitate reciproca, utraque facultas conservet sua jura illaesa in proprio activitatis campo."

Does this really solve our difficulty? There still remains the question of how the will can suddenly intervene in a series of *judicia practica* and blindly, as it were, makes one of them an *ultimo practicum*. Can we still speak of the reasonableness of free choice, if free choice means: (*voluntas*) *"immediate post aliquod judicium rationis ponit actum electionis, non exspectando ulterius aliud judicium rationis"*? This merely postpones the problem. For we must now ask ourselves how this intervention of the will, which makes the *judicium practicum* an *ultimum*, can be a rational one.

Only one answer remains possible. A series of *judicia practica* are made concerning a single object. Through an intervention of the spirit one of these *judicia practica* becomes a *judicium ultimo practicum*. Nevertheless this intervention of the spirit is neither a pure act of the free will nor a pure act of the understanding; it is rather a totality whose components are an act of the intellect and an act of the will. These two elements, the cognitive and the volitional act, are *natura simul* and mutually constitute each other. The totality which arises from these two elements is the free decision, the *electio libera*. The free decision is rational because it is also an act of the understanding. It is free because it arises from the spontaneity of the spirit without necessity. Both elements, the cognitive and the volitional, mutually cause each other. The intellectual elements, i.e. the *judicium ultimo practicum*, is an *ultimum* insofar as it is caused by an appetite. The volitional element, i.e. the free act of the will, is free, yet still rational, insofar as it is determined by the *judicium ultimo practicum*. Both can and indeed must mutually condition and cause each other since both are absolutely *natura simul* and essentially ordered to each other. They are as acts not things. They are *principia quibus* of which a concrete totality is composed.

The objection might be raised at this point that our explanation is not scholastic. For according to the scholastic tradition freedom is *formaliter* a property of the will. In our explanation however it is an attribute of understanding and will. To this objection we reply that, in the first place, scholasticism has always emphasized that both the will and the understanding have a share in the origin of the free election. If scholasticism teaches that freedom is *formaliter* in the will, it also teaches that freedom is *virtualiter* in the understanding. Scholasticism also teaches that the rationality of free choice is *formaliter* in the understanding and *virtualiter* in the will. Furthermore the proposition that freedom is to be ascribed *formaliter* to the will should not be taken to mean that only the will can be called the cause in the proper sense of the final, ultimate and decisive moment in the free election. Although scholastics speak here of *formaliter*, they give us to understand that a formal and a material element should be distinguished. Matter and form are intrinsic causes which are found *natura simul* in relation to one another and which mutually constitute each other.

If we then ask what is the form in the free decision and what is the matter, our answer, in accordance with tradition, will be that the will is the form and the understanding the matter. Or to put it more exactly, the will is the form and the understanding is the matter of freedom.

On the other hand however, we will also answer, in accordance with tradition, that so far as the rationality of
freedom goes, the understanding is the form and the will is
the matter. The will is the form of freedom, because freedom means first of all dynamic spontaneity; and the will is
dynamism which transcends the limits of pure knowledge.
Because the will means primarily dynamic spontaneity, it is
the form of freedom: *libertas est formaliter in voluntate.*
The matter of freedom is the understanding. The understanding is that which is determined by the movement of
the will. We must however look at the other side of the
situation also. The rationality of freedom is *formaliter* in
the understanding. Here the will is the matter which is
determined by a form.

Let us now summarize what has been said so far. The
old scholastic question about the rationality of the free election can be solved without contradiction only if we admit
that an act of the understanding and an act of the will are
mutually dependent on one another and so mutually constitute each other. Only in this way can we explain both
the rationality and the freedom of the free election.

Thus we have shown that there is an *a priori* of personal
being. There is a "free knowledge," a form of knowledge
which, *natura simul* with the will constitutes the free decision. In an analogous way then the cognitional moment of
the free decision is free and, in a corresponding way, the
volitional moment is rational.

That this type of knowledge is different from other forms
of knowledge, i.e. from intuitive and abstract-discursive
knowledge, needs no extensive proof. Personal knowledge is

the form of knowledge which constitutes the free choice together with the will insofar as it determines the will and
admits of determination by the will. It is different in structure therefore from every type of knowledge which is not
a partial element of the free decision.

Consequently, there are three levels of intellectual cognition, each of which is essentially distinct from the others:
intuitive knowledge, abstract-discursive knowledge and personal knowledge.

C.   The Essence of Personal Knowledge

1. *Free Knowledge.*   The free decision is a personal attitude, an attitude involving the total man. In a personal
attitude a determined relationship arises between the person
of the willing subject and the object. The Ego places itself
and the Other on the level of personal being, on the level of
personal freedom, which includes both necessity as well as
non-necessity.

The decision of the Ego does not concern the essence
or existence of a determined object present to it here and
now. The decision of the Ego concerns itself. I determine
myself. In the decision the Ego relates itself to the Other
and determines itself in relation to the Other. Through this
self-determination of the Ego, which takes place in every decision, the Other become a partial element of the personal
life of the Ego. For as object of the decision it is a partial
element of a personal attitude, and as such it becomes a
partial element of the truly personal life of the Ego.

As we have already seen, the free decision contains a volitional and a cognitive element. The formal act of the will which forms the volitional element of the free decision is the formal bearer of liberty. The cognitive element of the free choice, on the other hand, is the form of knowledge which is capable of knowing the object exhaustively in its new relationship. In this form of knowledge the other is known not only "objectively" but also "subjectively." It is not simply the Other, but the Other insofar as it is a partial element of the Ego and therefore shares in its "I-ness."

In the free decision the object is incorporated into the personal life of the Ego. This incorporation, insofar as it concerns mere things, need interest us no further at the moment. The formal elements of its essence are always the same. A determined other, whether it be thing, plant or animal, is incorporated into my personal life as "existing-for-me." This means that it is considered either as a means to something else in the proper sense of the word or simply as an element in my personal cosmos. But how does this incorporation of the Other into my personal life take place when I determine myself in relation to him through a decision about a personal Thou? What happens when a man in his free decision finds himself confronted with another man?

If I am in the presence of a man and know him, I form an intuition of which he is the content. In this intuition everything that I know of him is represented in one total image, and so he is known intuitively as a person. Yet this intuition of the other person remains an objective act of the understanding; it is neither immediately free knowledge, nor is it personal knowledge in the proper sense. If I should make a decision however touching this person, and in my free decision I assume a personal attitude toward him, then all that was contained in my intuition becomes, through my free decision, personal knowledge. Personal knowledge (if we consider it superficially) is a medium through which no more is received than was already contained in the intuition prior to it. All that is added to the intuition by it is the incorporation of the Other into the personal sphere of the Ego. If this intuition of the other person becomes personal knowledge, the Thou is incorporated into the personal life of the Ego and is known in it as such.[70]

But this incorporation of the Other into the personal life of the Ego, which constitutes the inner core of the free decision, is nothing other than a personal attitude toward the Other. If then the intuition of another person becomes personal knowledge in the free decision, an attitude of the whole person toward this determined individual is always taken up. Personal knowledge is precisely the cognitive element of this free attitude of the whole person toward this Thou. Prescinding from the multitude of distinctions which can be drawn between its various degrees, we must say that a cognitive attitude toward another Thou which is both personal and free can come into being in only one of two ways. It must be either positive or negative. That is to say, we either accept the Thou in his concrete personal being or we reject him. The first attitude is interpersonal faith; the second is unbelief.

If then a person comes to a free decision regarding another person and says "yes" to a Thou with the force of his

[70] E. Coreth, *Metaphysik als Aufgabe*, 80–95.

whole person, then in and through this decision our intuition is transformed into personal knowledge in which the other person is acknowledged as a Thou who has entered into my own personal life. The personal act of faith is thus the cognitive moment of a free attitude in which the Ego determines itself in relation to a Thou, insofar as it says "yes" to a Thou.

2. *Personal and Pre-Personal Knowledge.* Personal knowledge is, like every other knowledge, the being-present-to-itself of an existent. It is that intrinsic luminousness of the spirit by means of which it is not only conscious of itself as "present to itself," but through which it can also extend out beyond itself and bring the Other to its perfection within itself. But personal knowledge, as we have seen already in our phenomenological analysis, is essentially distinct from other forms of knowledge.

It is distinguished from the concept because it is not primarily abstract but is, on the contrary, concrete. It is distinct from the concept also because logical truth is found in it and therefore it must be related to a definite object; and because it is a medium through which we grasp not just some aspect of the existent but the existent itself in its unity and in its concrete plenitude of meaning and significance. Personal knowledge also differs from the judgment and from reasoning, for it is not divided into subject, predicate and copula. Just as in the intuition everything is contained within it in a single, undivided glance. Still personal knowledge is different in its structure from the previously described intuition. For the intuition is not, as is personal knowledge, a partial moment of a free attitude of the total person. And so it does not grasp the individual as an element of the free personal life of the Ego insofar as it is being lived at this very moment.

The essential note of personal knowledge is that it is free. It is free not merely in the sense that it is the object of a free decision. In this sense even an intuition, a judgment or concept can be free. For the individual can freely decide whether he wants to think or not. He can freely divert his understanding from an object or he can direct it toward an object. Personal knowledge is free in a more profound and immediate sense. It is a partial element of personal decision itself. Indeed personal knowledge is always an element of free self-determination. It is not merely "object"; it is "subject," a constitutive element of the Ego itself. Thus the freedom of personal knowledge is more immediate and more original than the freedom of any judgment or concept. It is the specific element of personal knowledge through which it is distinguished from all other forms of knowledge.

Human knowledge however is "with-the-Other." It is knowledge which is tied up with matter and whose origin is in the realm of the material. Human cognition is a *reditio completa ad se ipsum*, which has its beginning in the Other. It comes from without because it is sensible knowledge.

This conditions the temporal series of the different *a priori* functions. The object is grasped by the sensibility and actuated as the "*pantasma.*" This "phantasm" is spiritualized by the power of the *intellectus agens*; this means that it is grasped as a whole by the spirit and actuated as intuition. From the phantasm arises the intuition, the undivided vision of the object, a medium through which we grasp it at once as a concrete being and as a universal in its ontological relations. This intuition is the starting point of our intellectual knowledge.

From the intuition general aspects are abstracted, and thus we have the concept. When concepts are related to one another and to the reality grasped through the medium of the intuition, then we have the judgment. From many judgments we get a system.

From the intuition arises also personal knowledge. For the existent known through it must be incorporated into the personal sphere of the Ego. The Ego no longer encounters the Other in pure knowledge. The Other is actuated in his being-for-me. He becomes an object of my free attitude. And so from intuitive knowledge we get personal knowledge in the proper sense.

3. *Increase in Knowledge.* Between intuitive and personal knowledge we find the *a priori* function of personal being which elevates the pre-personal intuition to the higher and more perfect level of personal knowledge.

Just as the *intellectus agens* causes an increase of ontological perfection in the *species sensibilis* by producing from it a *species intelligibilis,* so too does the *a priori* of personal being with respect to the pre-personal intuition. The intuition is raised to a higher level of being, and therefore becomes more ontologically perfect and more interior to the Ego.

This necessitates however an increase in knowledge. In other words, personal knowledge means an increase in knowledge as opposed to the pre-personal intuition from which it took its origin. For an increase in being means always an increase in knowledge. Knowledge is indeed the being-present-to-itself of Being. Or expressed in scholastic terms, a more perfect *forma cognitionis* means a higher cognition. Because the *a priori* of personal being raises the prepersonal intuition to a higher level of being, the intuition becomes personal knowledge, that is, a higher, more interior, more perfect cognition. This is the increase in knowledge which we call the natural light of faith—that interior light of personal being which we always feel without being capable of grasping it conceptually. For only in this light of faith are the properly personal qualities of the Thou known in their full intelligibility. The transconceptual cannot however be grasped in concepts without being deprived of its own essence. This is the reason why the believer is the true judge of men. This is also why only faith can do justice to a personal Thou. Faith shows itself therefore to be the culmination of human knowledge.

3   Personal Faith

From what was said in the previous chapter it is clear that in addition to the concept, the judgment and discursive thought, and in addition to intuitive thought, there is still another level of intellectual knowledge which is structurally different from the other two. This is properly personal knowledge. It was pointed out that in the free decision the cognitive and volitional elements are absolutely *natura simul* without their being identical and that they mutually constitute each other. The cognitive element of the free decision which is related to a person as to its object is called faith or unbelief.

We have still to consider the object of faith, its certainty,

truth and motive. Through their consideration we will be
able to determine the nature of the *praeambula fidei* on
which our faith is grounded.

A. THE OBJECT OF FAITH

The object of personal faith is always and necessarily a Thou.
For only in the free attitude of our whole person toward another person is faith possible. By person we do not mean
here an abstract concept. We are not on the level of abstract-discursive thought, but on the level of personal knowledge where we are dealing always with the concrete plenitude
of being. By person therefore we mean here this concrete man, Peter, with all his virtues and vices, with his
sanguine temperament and with his sincerely warm glance.
This and only this is intended when we say that the object
of faith is the person: the Thou in his concrete human fullness.

And yet this determination of the object of belief is still
too general. To this general determination something else
must still be added: the holding-for-true of the assertions
of this Thou. For what a man says, particularly if it deals
with himself and with his personal states, belongs essentially
to the concrete Thou. His statements are self-revelations of
the Thou. They are its expression, and so also are elements
of the Thou itself. The believer, who says "yes" in faith to
a human Thou in his concrete fullness, will also say "yes"
to his assertions and accept them, for he takes them to be
true. This is the specific element of the object of faith.

Saying "yes" to the Thou in free knowledge, and accepting his assertions as true, are therefore not disparate realities. If we call the one "faith in a Thou" and the other "faith in an assertion," we can say that the faith in a Thou is related to faith in an assertion as a generic concept to a specific difference. The faith in a Thou is the more universal and more comprehensive concept which only receives its final form if it is specified by a particular difference. Faith in an assertion, on the contrary, reveals its true reality only when it is seen against the background of faith in a Thou.

It is evident that there are no clear-cut distinctions between faith in a Thou and faith in an assertion. For there is more in faith in an assertion than the explicitly formulated statement to which it gives assent. In it is also contained implicitly and tacitly, as something to which assent is also given, the meaningful activity of the man whom we believe. Faith in an assertion therefore is a concept whose rich content need not be added to, for it passes over into faith in a person in the proper sense.

If we should try to express this in traditional terminology then we would have to say: both the ontic reality of the concrete Thou and his assertions belong to the object of the act of faith.

B. The Truth of Faith

Since the act of faith is the cognitive element of the free decision and is therefore itself a type of knowledge, we must inquire into the truth of faith, and this means, of course, into the truth of both the faith in a Thou and faith in an assertion. This question is considerably more difficult than

it appears to be at first glance. Therefore we shall first have
to ask in what way the concept of truth can be applied to
the different levels of intellectual knowledge.

The neo-scholastic definitions of logical truth are not
completely uniform. Some of them are extremely general,
as, for example: *veritas est adequatio intellectus et rei.*[71]
Others, on the contrary, although they contain the same
basic elements, are more precise and to all appearances more
in conformity with the facts. Such, for example, would be
the definition which de Vries gives in his treatise on epistemology: *conformitas intellectus ad rem, inquantum intellectus dicit esse quod est, vel non esse quod non est.*[72] Nevertheless this definition cannot be used as easily as it would
first appear. For if it is to be applied universally, it must of its
very nature be verified in all true knowledge. Yet this is not
the case. For an intuition is, as we have already seen, an act of
knowledge containing formal truth (*continet veritatem
formalem*), and still it would not be correct to say of a true
intuition that there is in it a *conformitas intellectus ad rem,
inquantum intellectus dicit esse quod est, vel non esse quod
non est.* For in the intuition there is no "saying" in the proper
sense of the word since the intuition is an undivided vision.
Obviously, the second part of this definition of truth has
been drawn up to fit the structure of the judgment in which
there is really a *dicit esse quod est, vel non esse quod non
est.* In the intuition, on the other hand, there is nothing of
the sort.

[71] This is the definition generally employed in the middle ages.
We shall see that it is in conformity with reality.
[72] J. de Vries, *Critica*, no. 25

This difficulty with the neo-scholastic definition becomes still clearer if we ask what is the truth of the *judicium practicum*. This is, to be sure, an act of knowledge which of its essence is always and necessarily either true or false. What then is the truth of such a *judicium practicum?* De Vries endeavors to answer by showing that his definition is verified even in the *judicium practicum*. For every *judicium practicum*, says de Vries, depends on what truly is. The *judicium practicum* depends on determined norms with which it must be in conformity. These norms however are an *esse*, and so it follows that, even in the *judicium practicum*, truth can be defined as *conformitas intellectus ad rem, inquantum.* . . .[73]

De Vries' reasoning is clearly conclusive so long as we are dealing with *judicia practica* which express an obligation. For all judgments which express an obligation presuppose either the natural law or a positive decree on the part of a lawgiver. In such a case there is actually *conformitas intellectus ad rem, inquantum.* . . . Not all *judicia practica* however express an obligation. If, for example, we are to assume a free attitude toward a person, or if we are to come to a decision, we must form a *judicium practicum* (we would say an intuition). This *judicium practicum*, as we have already seen, is *natura simul* with the volitional element of the free decision. We can then ask where the traditional definition of truth is verified. Is there in this case a *conformitas intellectus ad rem?* Or is there even a *dicit esse quod est* at all? We are confronted here with a free decision, a *judicium practicum* from which a state of affairs comes into being for

[73] *Ibid.* no. 289.

the first time. In and through the free decision and therefore through this *judicium practicum*, I bring into being a
personal relationship to another person. This personal relationship does not exist prior to the *judicium practicum*; it is
constituted in the free decision and in the *judicium practicum*. We cannot maintain therefore that we have here a
*conformitas intellectus ad rem, inquantum intellectus dicit
esse quod est, vel non esse quod non est*. It would be much
more correct for us to say: *adaequatio intellectus et rei, inquantum intellectus simul cum voluntate ita dicit esse, ut
fiat*.

How can we apply the traditional definition to a *judicium
practicum*, if the *judicium practicum* is not merely the intellectual assimilation of an object, but, far more than that, the
projection of something new, the projection of a personal
relationship? From what has been said above, we can see
that the customary scholastic definition of truth is not as
free from difficulties as it is often assumed to be. Neo-
scholastic philosophy and, to some extent, neo-scholastic
theology also operate principally on the level of abstractive-
discursive thought. On this level on which the judgment is
the bearer of truth, it is completely correct to say *veritas est
adaequatio intellectus et rei, quatenus intellectus dicit esse
quod est, vel non esse quod non est*. But there are other
levels of intellectual thought as well on which we find acts
of knowledge which contain formal truth. If we are to do
justice to this fact, we must go back to the old scholastic
definition of truth which says: *veritas est adaequatio intellectus et rei*. This generic definition which classical scholasticism has handed down to us can be applied in every in-

stance in which an act of knowledge contains formal truth. It need only to be specified in more detail, in conformity to the kind of knowledge we are dealing with. If we limit it to the judgment, we must say: *veritas judicii est adaequatio intellectus et rei, quatenus intellectus dicit esse quod est, vel non esse quod non est.* If the definition is applied to the intuition then it must run: *veritas intuitionis est adaequatio intellectus et rei, quatenus intellectus videt esse, quod est.*

If we ask how truth must be defined when we limit it to the level of personal knowledge, then the matter becomes essentially more difficult. For the cognitive element of the personal attitude is formally an act of cognition, and must therefore be either true or false. The multiplicity of aspects which are simultaneously in operation here forbids us however to set down a short, simple, specific definition. The intuition is very simply structured, and so we are able to frame our definition of it without much difficulty. It is applicable to all intuitions and to intuitions only. With personal knowledge, on the other hand, the situation is quite different. There are several kinds of personal knowledge which differ in structure from each other. We cannot therefore combine them under a common name without more ado. All we can do then is to enumerate some of the most important forms of personal knowledge and then try to discover what is "their" specific truth.

There is a personal knowledge whose exclusive content is an obligation accepted by the knower. Such, for example, would be the case were a man to come to a free personal decision to act in accordance with the natural law. This personal knowledge, which is the cognitive element of the deci-

sion, contains two elements: knowledge of the natural law
and the personal relation which comes into being from the
fact that the person freely assents to this obligation. These
two elements are not only contained in the free decision;
they are also contained specifically in its cognitive element.
For the cognitive element of this free decision is not merely
knowledge of the moral law; it is also the cognitive affirmation which belongs essentially to the volitional as well as the
cognitive moment of a personal attitude. These two elements however are different in the character of their truth.
Knowledge of the natural moral law is a knowledge which
presupposes its object as a given reality. The truth that we
find here then is *adaequatio intellectus et rei, quatenus intellectus videt esse quod est.* In other words, this knowledge
of the natural law which is given intuitively in personal
knowledge is true or false depending on whether or not it
truly represents the objective reality of the moral law. The
second element of this personal knowledge however is completely different in the character of its truth. For this personal relation to the natural law, this cognitive affirmation
which people call recognition, is not something already
given prior to the free decision and to its cognitive element.
It is something which becomes what it is only in and
through personal knowledge (and through the free decision). We must say therefore that in this case the truth is
nothing other than *adaequatio intellectus et rei, quatenus
intellectus (et voluntas) libere ponit esse ita, ut fiat.* We
have here something analogous to the truth which belongs
to the divine creative power. The object of knowledge is not
"received" or "grasped"; it is projected into the order of
reality for the first time in its own proper being.

There is moreover a personal knowledge which contains no obligation. Such would be the case, for example, were I to make a free decision to take a stroll. The personal knowledge which is part of this free decision does not grasp an object but projects it. Nonetheless we have here, at least implicitly, knowledge of something already given. For this personal knowledge which projects the concrete stroll as the stroll I now assent to presupposes at least as already given the general structure of a stroll. These few rather insignificant components of personal knowledge have a receptive truth character: *videt esse quod est.* In these instances, it must be admitted, the *esse quod est* is reduced to an abstract structure or even to an abstract possibility. Perhaps it will be said at this point that the last-named type of truth is the primary one. Personal knowledge possesses in the first place a receptive type of truth which presupposes its object as a given. The projective type of truth is merely a secondary one. Such an opinion however cannot be squared with the phenomena. Why can we not say that the projective type truth is the primary and central element of personal knowledge? The creative knowledge of God, the scholastic *scientia visionis,* also has a receptive type of truth insofar as the *scientia visionis* presupposes and somehow includes the *scientia intelligentis.* Nevertheless the *scientia visionis* possesses a projective type of truth. Why can we not say that the same thing is true in an analogous sense of the case we are considering now?

We could enumerate still other types of personal knowledge, but, were we to do so, we would be brought back in every case to the same general structure. Personal knowledge always possesses this twofold type of truth. We can therefore give the many types of personal knowledge a common name, and so define the truth of personal knowledge in its specific nature somewhat as follows: *adaequatio intellectus et rei, quatenus intellectus partim videt esse quod est, partim (cum voluntate) ponit esse ita, ut fiat.* This definition, to be sure, is not completely simple; but the difficulty lies in the object, and so is unavoidable.

We are now in a position to determine the specific nature of the truth we find in interpersonal faith. Since we are dealing with personal knowledge, the above-mentioned double type of truth manifests itself. Insofar as it is an intuitive vision of a person therefore faith has a merely receptive character. It presupposes the object as something given: *adaequatio intellectus et rei, quatenus intellectus videt esse quod est.* However, insofar as it brings a personal relation into being, i.e. insofar as it adopts a cognitive attitude toward a person, faith has truth of the projective type: *adaequatio intellectus et rei, quatenus intellectus (cum voluntate) ponit esse ita, ut fiat.*

If we now apply what we have discovered to the concepts "faith in a Thou" and "faith in an assertion," we can draw the following conclusions. Faith in a Thou possesses both types of truth, for it includes both the intuitive, receptive vision of a person and the cognitive "yes" we say to him.

It might be said that faith in an assertion has only one type of truth—receptive truth. For faith in an assertion is simply the holding-to-be-true of the statements of a Thou. If these statements are true, then the holding-to-be-true of the assertions is also an act of knowledge which is true. Nevertheless this is not the case. Faith in an assertion also

possesses both types of truth, the receptive and the projective. We must not forget that faith in an assertion is not
an independent act, but rather a partial element of a single
act. Faith in an assertion is included in the "yes" which we
say to the statements of a person. If I say "yes" to a Thou
in his concreteness, then I say "yes" as well to the assertions
which form a peripheral element of his concreteness. Since
faith in an assertion is only one aspect of faith in the proper
sense, it possesses also the same twofold character as the
act of faith itself. When "yes" is said also to the statements of a Thou as well as to his person, we have then projective truth as well as receptive truth; and there is also
something which is projected: my personal relation to these
statements. As a matter of fact, these statements are not accepted simply intellectually; they are accepted personally.
And when "yes" is said by a person this always implies the
bringing of a personal relation in being.

C.   The Certitude of Faith

1.   *Two Questions Are to be Asked:* what is the certitude
of faith? Whence does this certitude arise? The answer to
the second question is essentially dependent on our answer
to the first. The question concerning the nature of the certitude of faith is not however as simple as we might assume
at first glance. We have to deal here with the same difficulty
which occupied us in the previous section: that the concept
of certitude as it is generally understood by scholastic philosophers and theologians does not appear to be univocal.

The concept of certitude, and the concept of truth as

well, is derived in contemporary scholasticism through an analysis of the structure of judgment. The definition acquired in this way however is still not universal enough, with the result that, practically speaking, it can only be applied to the judgment itself. Thus, for example, Heinrich Lennerz, when he is dealing as a theologian with the certitude of faith, is compelled to give a definition of certitude which is completely at variance with the one proposed by de Vries in his treatise on epistemology.[74]

To avoid this equivocacy of its present-day scholastic concept, we must try to define certitude in such a way that our definition can be applied not only to the judgment, but also to faith and to all types of knowledge in which certitude is found. Then our generic definition of certitude can be made more precise by adapting it to the type of knowledge to which it is applied.

The syllogism and the judgment, the intuition or personal knowledge are all either true or false. Each of these individual types of knowledge can be endowed with certitude. It is important to disinguish between these types of perfect knowledge in which *veritas formalis* is found and the concept which is neither true nor false.

Let us prescind from the content of an act of perfect knowledge in order to consider it simply in its formal structure and insofar as it is an interior "yes," an assent or an affirmation. Knowledge understood in this sense we shall call knowledge of affirmation, or in scholastic terminology *assensus formaliter sumptus*. Knowledge of affirmation can

[74] H. Lennerz, *De virtutibus theologicis*, Rome 1933, 3rd ed., 126–127

be firm. This firmness in knowledge of affirmation (*assensus firmus*) we shall call subjective certitude. If however the knowledge of affirmation is not only "firm," but more than that, "unalterable in and for itself," then we have a formal (i.e. subjective-objective) certitude (*certitudo formaliter sumpta*). By formal certitude we understand therefore an *assensus firmus et per se immutabilis*.

This definition of formal certitude, which is much closer to the teaching of classical scholasticism than it is to the definition commonly used by the neo-scholastics, is applicable to every act of knowledge endowed with certitude, i.e. to all knowledge which involves certitude. For both the syllogism and the judgment, as well as the intuition (evidence) and the act of belief, are acts of knowledge which imply an *assensus firmus et per se immutabilis*. If we wished however to define certitude as *assensus firmus in evidentia fundatus*, then indeed we would have given a description of the type of certitude which is peculiar to the judgment. This is actually an *assensus firmus in evidentia fundatus*. But this is not a definition of certitude in general. For evidence is also knowledge, knowledge which contains truth; and accordingly it is also knowledge which possesses certitude. How shall this type of certitude be defined? Not as *assensus firmus IN EVIDENTIA FUNDATUS*. The same can be said for the act of faith. The act of faith is an act of knowledge possessing formal truth; yet nevertheless its truth is not an *assensus firmus in evidentia fundatus*, since the believer possesses no evidence for the fact to which his assent is given.

We now ask whence this certitude arises. What can be

its ground as an *assensus firmus et per se immutabilis?* The
first answer which we must give to this question is not
difficult. The *assensus* is *firmus et per se immutabilis* because it is an *assensus* which possesses truth. For formal
truth implies not only an *adaequatio intellectus et rei,* but,
more than this, it implies also consciousness of this *adaequatio.* The knowing subject therefore who gives an *assensus firmus et per se immutabilis* can do so because in
this *assensus* there is contained a conscious *adaequatio intellectus et rei.* In other words, the certitude of knowledge
is due to the fact that there is in it an awarness of its own
possession of truth. Thus we have come into possession of
a principle which admittedly says little enough in its formal
abstractness, but which nonetheless can be applied to all
knowledge possessing formal truth. The certitude of knowledge is due in the first place to its formal truth. Still this
does not bring us much further, for we now have to ask
what is the origin of this complexus of truth and certitude
in knowledge. To answer this question we shall have to inquire into the origin of this complexus in each type of certain knowledge.

2. In the syllogism, or even in discursive thought in
general, the conclusion is an act of knowledge which possesses certitude. This means that it is an act of knowledge
which possesses both formal truth and certitude. We already know that the certitude of this conclusion is grounded
in the first place consciously by possessed truth (*veritas
formalis*) which it contains. Now we ask a further question. What is the origin of this formal truth?

The answer to this question is given to us in a principle

of classical logic. The truth of the conclusion depends exclusively on the truth of the premises (presupposing that the form of the syllogism is correct). Another classical law states that the certitude of the conclusion is no greater than the certitude of the least certain premise: *pejorem sequitur semper conclusio partem.*[75] Thus classical logic gives us first a negative answer to our question. The truth and certitude of a conclusion are not absolute properties of this conclusion. Yet there is even more to be said. For if these properties of the conclusion are not absolute but relative properties, then they are dependent on something else which is not identical with them. And the first-named logical principle shows precisely what it is on which the truth and the certitude of the conclusion depends, i.e. the truth and certitude of the premises. Yet the premises of a syllogism are judgments, and so we are forced to say that the truth and certitude of a conclusion depend on the truth and certitude of those judgments which serve as its premises. This dependence is a logical one. In other words, its nature is exactly as the laws of logic show it to be.

We have seen then that the source of truth and certitude in the conclusion is the same as the source of the truth and certitude in the determined judgments which are its premises. This however simply moves our inquiring into their source back a step, for we must now inquire into the source of the truth and certitude of the judgment.

The scholastic theory of cognition answers this question by saying that the evidence is the ground of the truth and certitude of the *judicium certum.* We have already gone

---

[75] J. de Vries, *Logica*, no. 250

into the exact meaning of this answer in our preceding discussion concerning intuition and its relationship to the judgment. At this point then we need only refer to our previous conclusion. The judgment is simply an intuition broken down into subject, predicate and copula. The intuition is "evidence" with respect to the judgment. The knowing subject can, for example, make the judgment *homo est animal rationale* because he sees in the intuition that this relation is "truly in the thing," that it is conformed to reality. The intuition is therefore an act of knowledge from which the knowing subject derives through analysis the various components of the judgment. If however everything which is contained in the judgment comes from the intuition, then the truth and certitude of the judgment also have their source in the intuition. This is also the teaching of the epistemologists when they propose evidence as the ground or foundation of the truth and certitude of the judgment. Nevertheless our answer is still not completely satisfying. We know that the truth and the certitude of the judgment depend on the intuition. But what is the nature of this dependence?

The dependence of the judgment's truth and certitude on evidence is described by epistemologists, if they inquire into the matter at all, in more or less the following terms: *exprimendo id, quod evidens est, dico esse, quod est, i.e. vere judico;*[76] or *evidentia ergo relate ad veritatem est "criterium," i.e. mensura, ad quam comparatum enuntiabile cognoscitur ut verum.*[77] This means that the dependence of

[76] J. de Vries, Critica, no. 137.
[77] Ibid. no. 25

the judgment's truth and certitude on the intuition is of the type which we call "logical." It is true, of course, that in this instance we cannot speak of logical laws in the strict sense. Such laws are valid only for discursive thought. Basically however in this case too we are dealing with the same principle. The truth of the judgment depends wholly on the truth of the intuition and, therefore, certitude of the judgment can be no greater than the certitude of the intuition. This statement is in complete agreement with the phenomena, for if something given in evidence as only "probable" is affirmed as "certain" in the judgment, such a judgment is always false. In other words, it is no longer conformed to reality. This is also in conformity with the structure of the judgment demanded by the metaphysics of knowledge, for in the judgment we find knowledge that is clearer in some respects (because of its abstractness), but knowledge that is by no means more perfect in all respects. The certitude of the judgment cannot be any greater than the certitude of the intuition.

3. *What then is the source* of the truth of the intuition? Whence comes its certitude? After all that we have seen in our previous chapter on the nature and cause of the intuition, one answer alone is possible. The truth and certitude of the intuition have their origin in sensation. They are derived, in other words, from the *phantasm*. The intuition is simply a spiritualized phantasm, a *species intelligibilis*. It arises from the phantasm alone, under the influence of the *intellectus agens*; it has no other source whatever.

Through this answer, which has diverted our discussion from the central point of the problem, we have brought ourselves up against another and quite difficult problem. How can the truth and certitude of the intuition be dependent on the phantasm? The truth of the phantasm is by no means formal truth; it is purely material truth in which the *adaequatio inter cognoscentem et rem* is not known at all. The certitude of the phantasm moreover is a *certitudo mere sensibilis,* which is essentially less perfect than the intellectual certitude possessed by the intuition. How then can we still claim that the truth and certitude of the intuition are dependent on the phantasm?

Truth and certitude in the intuition have their origin in the phantasm insofar as the intuition itself is abstracted from the phantasm. This relation of dependence however is by no means a logical one. By this we mean that although the intuition and its truth and certitude are ontologically dependent on the phantasm in their origin, they are not "logically" dependent on it. Thus there is no logical dependence of any kind. In principle therefore any attempt to apply to this case the logical laws which we mentioned previously must be ruled out. We cannot therefore consider the phantasm as a sort of premise and the intuition as a conclusion, and say concerning them: *pejorem sequitur semper conclusio partem.* The reason for this is very simple. The relationship of dependence which exists between the intuition and the phantasm is completely different from the logical dependence of the conclusion on its premises. The reason for this difference is revealed by the metaphysics of knowledge which has disclosed the presence of an ontological *a priori* (the *intellectus agens*) between the phantasm and the intuition. This *a priori* transforms the sensible phantasm into an essentially more perfect spiritual intuition.

Thus we have once more regained the traditional teaching. For the philosophy of the schools teaches that the "evidence" (we call it intuition), although it is ontologically dependent on the phantasm in its origin, is not logically dependent on it. More than that, we have gained some important insights. We now know that it is fundamentally possible for an act of knowledge to be ontologically dependent on another in its origin without being logically dependent on it. We know too that in such a case it is impossible of the very nature of the case to apply the laws of logic and so say with relation to its certitude: *pejorem sequitur semper conclusio partem.* We have also seen that the metaphysical reason why logical dependence is excluded on principle is the fact that between the one act of knowledge and the other there exists an *a priori* through whose casual influence an essentially more perfect act of knowledge can arise from a less perfect one.

Still our question has not yet been answered. We know indeed that the intuition arises ontologically from the phantasm. We know that it is logically not dependent on it. But on what is it logically dependent? Our answer is that the intuition is not logically dependent on any other act of knowledge. In fact, this question concerning a "logical whence" is out of place. For the basic presupposition behind such a question is that every act of knowledge, whatever it may be, must be logically dependent on another. This reasoning is false however and would lead to a *processus in infinitum,* for if this were so there would be no logically independent knowledge. And this is reason enough to show quite clearly that there must be an act of knowledge which is logically independent of any other act of knowledge.

Must every intuition however be such a logically independent act of knowledge? Would it not be enough if there were a greater or lesser number of intuitions which were logically independent? Again we must answer in the negative. For the logical independence of the intuition is given with the nature of the intuition itself. The intuition is indeed the first grade of spiritual knowledge and on it all other intellectual knowledge depends. The intuition however, as spiritualized phantasm, is dependent on the phantasm alone. It is ultimately directed, of course, to the judgment, to the syllogism and to personal knowledge, but in no way is it causally dependent on them (*secundum causam efficientem*). Therefore it cannot logically be dependent on them either, for logical dependence is simply causal dependence on the intentional level. Since the intuition is "logically" dependent neither on the phantasm nor on other acts of intellectual knowledge, it is necessarily "logically" independent. Therefore there is no logical source of truth and certitude in the intuition.

This falls in completely with the scholastic theory of evidence. Evidence derives its truth and certitude not from "outside" itself but from within itself.

One might object here that an epistemological inquiry into the source of the certitude of evidence is possible. Thus contemporary epistemologists endeavor to ground the truth and certitude of "mediate evidence" (by which they have in mind the spiritualized phantasm, and there the intuition). In reply we can say that there is a considerable difference between the process of grounding such evidence epistemologically and the natural operation of the mind. The spiritualized phantasm, the mediate evidence and therefore the intuition, which I possess of this table and this lamp, as such already possess truth and certitude. I know the table and the lamp and am certain of the conformity of my knowledge to reality—and all of this without having made any epistemological reflection on it. The certitude of the intuition (mediate evidence) then is not at all the conclusion of an epistemological consideration carried on by means of conceptual thought. It is an essential component of the intuition itself. If this were not the case, the certitude of an intuition would be always and of its very nature logically dependent on the certitude of an epistemological discursus. In that case the certitude which I have concerning this table and this lamp would never be greater than the certitude of my epistemological system, and anyone who held another epistemological system would not have the same certitude concerning this lamp and table. It is to do violence to reality therefore to make a reflection out of a process which in reality is nonconceptual. If one should still insist that there is such an epistemological discursus, we might well ask where it is, what is its nature, and why we have no experience of it. And if in answer someone should assert that there is in all men an identical, even though unconscious epistemological discursive process, we might ask as well why it is not possible for us to raise it to the level of consciousness, so that all men who desire to do so might possess the same epistemological system. These difficulties make it sufficiently clear that the scholastic position is the correct one. It is also the only one which does justice to the phenomena, for we experience the certitude of an intuition as something as immediate as the intuition itself and not as a product of conceptual thought. This is also unequivocally clear from what we have learned from the metaphysics of knowledge. The certitude of the intuition cannot be simply the product of a conceptual, epistemological reflection, since every conceptual discursus already presupposes the intuition, a fact which was established in some detail earlier in our discussion.

And so our question has been answered. As far as its truth and certitude are concerned, the intuition is dependent on the phantasm in its origin. This dependence is purely ontological. Logically, the intuition is in no way dependent on the phantasm. Thus there is no logical source of the intuition's truth and certitude.

4. We have now come to the level of personal knowledge, and we must endeavor to discover the source of its truth and certitude. On the basis of our previous discussion concerning the intuition we know that this generic question breaks down into two separate questions. We must endeavor to discover the ontological as well as the logical source of the truth and the certitude of personal knowledge.

The question about the ontological source of the certitude and truth of personal knowledge has really been answered already in what we have said above about the nature of the personal *a priori*. We have seen that personal knowledge comes into being when an intuition is incorporated into the act of free decision. The intuition becomes the cognitive moment of this free decision. The cognitive and volitional moments of the free decision mutually determine each other with the result that the decision is both free and rational. Since therefore the cognitive moment of the free decision is determined by the volitional moment (and vice versa), we must say that personal knowledge is determined ontologically and transcendentally by the volitional moment of the free decision. From what we have said, it follows then that the ontological source of personal knowledge is found in both the intuition and the volitional element of the free decision. Personal knowledge has the intuition as its ontological source in the volitional element of the free decision. Personal knowledge has the intuition as its ontological source insofar as it is pure cognition; it has its ontological source in the volitional element of the free decision insofar as it is *personal* knowledge whose certitude is consequently *free* certitude. Thus the question concerning the ontological source of personal knowledge has been answered.

We now must ask about the logical source of the truth and certitude of personal knowledge. Is it possible to consider personal knowledge the conclusion of even an implicit syllogism? Is personal knowledge such a conclusion of this sort? Can we say then of personal knowledge: *pejorem sequitur semper conclusio partem?* Can we say that the certitude of personal knowledge can never be greater than the certitude of the intuition from which it originated?

On the basis of what was seen in our phenomenological analysis, we must answer this question in the negative. In our introductory phenomenological analysis we saw that the certitude of personal faith—and faith is personal knowledge—is experienced in many cases as the firmest of all our certitudes. The certitude of personal faith from a phenomenological point of view is the highest point that certitude can reach. If this is the case, we cannot say that every act of personal knowledge in relation to its certitude is logically dependent on the intuition corresponding to it. For if this were so, the certitude of personal knowledge would not be the firmest of all certitudes. The evidence of our phenomenological analysis compels us to say therefore that there are many cases of personal knowledge in which it is logically independent of the intuition which is its ontological source.

This answer, based on purely phenomenological evidence, leaves us still unsatisfied, for it leaves too many points still unsettled, and it does not make clear why what we have seen must be so and cannot be otherwise. If we attempt to approach the problem from a metaphysical point of view, then we must recall what we proved above concerning the intuition. There we established through our analysis of the structure of the intuition the formal principle that the certitude of the intuition is logically independent of the certitude of sense knowledge because and insofar as there is an a priori between sense knowledge and the intuition which elevates the sensible phantasm to the essentially more perfect intuition. We raised this principle to the level of a general principle when we said that one act of knowledge is logically independent of another if there is between the two an a priori which elevates one act of knowledge to an essentially more perfect act of knowledge. This generalization is metaphysically necessary. For certitude is a property of an act of knowledge which is not really distinct from it. If therefore from an act of knowledge A an essentially more perfect act of knowledge B arises by virtue of an *a priori*, then this act of knowledge B, together with every property not really distinct from it, is essentially more perfect than act of knowledge A. Therefore it is absolutely impossible that certitude B logically depends on certitude A.

If we now apply this principle to our inquiry into the logical source of personal knowledge, we must say that there is no logical source of personal knowledge. It is logically dependent on no other act of knowledge. For between personal knowledge and the intuition (which is, of course, its source in the ontological order) there is an *a priori* which elevates the intuition to the essentially more perfect act of personal knowledge. For it is essentially more perfect; it is personal knowledge which springs from man's personal center; it is immediately (although not formally) free. It is always ordered to the most interior and central core of the person. It is moreover essentially more perfect than the intuition to which it corresponds, because an *a priori* has elevated it to an essentially more perfect form of knowledge. This *a priori* is the free decision itself, or put more precisely, it is that *a priori* from which the free decision originates. Personal knowledge becomes what it is for the first time in and through the free decision: an act of knowledge essentially more perfect than the intuition from which it was its ontological source. If this is the case, then we must say by virtue of the above-mentioned principle that personal knowledge is not logically dependent on any other act of knowledge. There is no logical source of personal knowledge, just as there is no logical source of the intuition.

Thus we have now answered the problem concerning the certitude of faith. There is, of course, an ontological source for the certitude of faith. It arises from the intuition and from the volitional moment of the free decision. But there is no logical source for the certitude of faith; it is logically dependent on no other act of knowledge. In no way then is it an act of knowledge of which we can say: *pejorem sequitur semper conclusio partem.*

There are however two aspects in the knowledge of faith. We have seen earlier that we can distinguish between faith in a Thou and faith in an assertion. Does what we have just said concerning the source of the certitude of faith apply in the same way to faith in a Thou and faith in an assertion? What we have seen above therefore will have to be more carefully distinguished before we can apply it accurately to both aspects of the act of faith.

Faith in an assertion is nothing else then the "yes" we say to a Thou, insofar as this assertion is included as an expression, as a peripheral element of the concrete personality of the Thou, in the "yes" we say to the Thou himself. From this it is evident that both the truth and the certitude of faith in an assertion have their immediate origin in the fact that the Thou himself is included in the "yes" which we utter in faith in a Thou. The believer often possesses no direct knowledge of the facts which are proposed in this assertion. If then he himself is certain of the truth of these assertions, then it can only be because they are, as it were, an ontal extension, peripheral components of the Thou himself.

Since the Thou is accepted in his concrete fullness in faith in a Thou, his statements are also accepted. The immediate logical source of the truth and certitude of faith in an assertion is accordingly faith in the Thou himself. Faith in a Thou however, as we have seen, has no logical source. Thus faith in an assertion is logically dependent on faith in a Thou. Since however faith in a Thou is logically independent of the intuition, faith in an assertion is logically independent of it also.

The objection may be raised that in this case faith in an assertion is totally without foundation. For the "yes" which we say to the Thou gives us no guarantee that his assertions are true, in which case there can be no certitude at all in faith in an assertion. This is not so however. For the "yes" which we say to the Thou is not a "yes" spoken to an abstract essence (*animal rationale*); it is rather a dynamic "yes" spoken to a concrete Thou, who with all his human virtues, and therefore his truthfulness, is the subject to whom the acceptance of this "yes" is given. Since we say "yes" to the Thou as a truthful man in faith in a Thou, faith in an assertion can be dependent on faith in a Thou. The logical source of certitude in faith in an assertion is consequently to be found in faith in a Thou. This source is the Thou in whom we have faith, insofar as he possesses knowledge and truthfully communicates it to us.

5. Let us now draw together the most important conclusions of the previous section in an attempt to summarize them, as far as possible, in scholastic terminology. We have discovered that there are two essentially distinct types of dependence: the certitude of an act of knowledge can be logically or ontologically dependent on another act of

knowledge. The essential note of logical dependence is its subjection to the logical law: *pejorem semper sequitur conclusio partem*, so that the certitude of an act of knowledge can be no greater than the certitude of the act of knowledge on which it is logically dependent. Ontological dependence, on the other hand, although it implies, to be sure, a metaphysical dependence of one act of knowledge on another, does not imply at all thereby that they must be equal in the degree of their certitude. For the certitude of an act of knowledge whose dependence on another is purely ontological is, because of the *a priori*, essentially higher and more perfect than the certitude of the act of knowledge from which it originated.

We call an act of knowledge on which another act of knowledge logically depends a motive. Looked at in the concrete therefore a motive is an act of knowledge on which another act is logically dependent. Formally considered, the motive is the source of certitude of a logically dependent act of knowledge. In other words, the motive is the ground or *ratio* because of which a logically dependent act of knowledge possesses certitude (*ratio propter quam dature assensus*).

If however one act of knowledge is not logically dependent on any other act of knowledge, it has no motive; it is logically independent. It is its own motive. We can then call it self-motivated. For an act of knowledge to have its own motive means therefore that the ground of its certitude is found in itself.

The outcome of our reflection then can be summed up as follows:

a)   Intuition is the motive for the judgment's certitude.

b)   The intuition however has no motive; it is its own motive.

c)   Faith in an assertion has as its motive faith in a Thou. Faith in a Thou as a motive means the Thou who possesses knowledge and truthfully communicates it, insofar as he is a subject to whom we say "yes" in faith in a Thou.

d)   Faith in a Thou has no motive; it is self-motivated.

e)   The intuition is in no way the motive of belief.

D.   The Degrees of Faith

The formal way in which we considered the *a priori* of faith caused us to pass over an important point which must now be discussed, i.e. the fundamental reason why there can be degrees in faith.

Our introductory phenomenological analysis of faith showed that there are several very distinct degrees of interpersonal faith. We also saw that both the certitude and the object of faith can be quite different. Where one man is concerned, we shall take his word only in regard to insignificant things, whereas where another is concerned we shall accept in all simplicity whatever he seriously proposes for our belief. One act of faith is endowed with a relatively slight degree of certitude; another, on the contrary, is more certain than any other act of knowledge.

What is the reason for the difference? Does it stem perhaps from the motive of faith? Could it be that the logical dependence of faith is normative in this respect?

We have already seen that the certitude of faith in an assertion is logically dependent on faith in a Thou. It is determined by faith in a Thou himself. If therefore there are

degrees of certitude in faith in an assertion, their origin must
be in a corresponding faith in a Thou which carries within
itself its own certitude. But what can be the origin of these
different degrees of certitude in faith in a Thou?

Faith in a Thou is not dependent on the intuition for its
own certitude. Consequently, the degrees of certitude in
faith in a Thou cannot arise from a corresponding gradation
in the certitude of intuition. We saw that there can be no
parallelism here, and that the principle *pejorem sequitur
semper condusio partem* is not applicable to this case. The
fact therefore that the intuition which precedes the act of
faith possesses certitude A has nothing to do with the fact
that faith in a Thou is endowed with certitude B. Their relationship is analogous to the relationship between the certitude of the phantasm and the intuition which originated
from it. The degree of certitude in this intuition is not determined simply by the phantasm, for the certitude of the
intuition is always and necessarily firmer and more perfect
than the certitude of the phantasm.

If then the degrees of belief in a Thou do not arise from
the intuition, what is their origin? Faith in a Thou admittedly arises from the intuition. We can say, analogically
speaking, that faith in a Thou is in relation to the intuition
what the intuition is in relation to the phantasm. Perhaps
however the degree of certitude in faith in a Thou is simply
due to the fact that the act of faith is the cognitive movement of a free attitude. Is it our free personal being—which
cannot be deduced from anything else—which we should
hold accountable for the variety in the degrees of faith?

Certainly the gradation in belief arises primarily from our

personal center. For without its personal being, faith, as a personal act, is inconceivable. Personal being implies freedom. Freedom implies not only the fundamental possibility of being able to say "yes" or "no," but more than that the possibility of saying "yes" in this way or in some other way.

Does this mean however that the variety in the degrees of faith is arbitrary? Clearly this is not so. For freedom is not arbitrariness. The fact that I can say "yes" or "no" to this concrete Thou and that I can utter this "yes" in this way or that does not mean that these fundamental possibilities are incomprehensible and so should be ascribed to blind arbitrariness. For even personal liberty, or rather we should say precisely this personal liberty, must be being; and being is present-to-itself. The fundamental possibilities which are fulfilled by the Ego in personal freedom are grounded in being and can therefore be conceived in the necessity which determines them as free possibilities. We must therefore trace the degrees of faith, which is given to another in personal freedom, back to the degrees of being, which, as they present themselves to freedom prior to its action, impose on it the determination of an ought.

These are the degrees of ontological perfection in the Thou. For the kind of "yes" which I utter to a Thou in faith should be in keeping with his ontological perfection. The ontological perfection of the Thou who becomes present to me through the medium of the intuition reveals itself as the ground of the fundamental possibility of diverse grades of certitude. The intuition is the ground of possibility for the degrees of certitude therefore not insofar as it is endowed with a determined grade of certitude, but insofar as it is the medium through which a Thou possessed of a determined ontological perfection becomes present to us.

The truth of this statement can be confirmed through a phenomenological reflection. Let us assume that I have an extremely detailed intuition of Peter in which the various facets of his character are very clearly distinguished. I have known Peter for many years. I know his character in all its different aspects. My long acquaintanceship with Peter has given me an intuition of him which has a very high degree of certitude. The intuition which I have of Peter then is endowed with the highest degree of moral certitude. But what is the content of this intuition? What kind of a person is Peter? He is a miserable man, utterly consumed with weaknesses and with vice. Briefly and bluntly, he cannot be trusted. Thus, although the intuition which I have of Peter has a very high certitude, its content tells me that Peter is "worthy of belief" only to a slight degree. If then from this intuition an act of faith arises, this faith will possess a very low degree of certitude. I will believe Peter only in insignificant matters. The certitude of this faith does not depend therefore on the formal certitude of the intuition, but rather on its content. The content of this intuition, i.e. the image of Peter, of which it is the medium, is the source of the definite grade of certitude which my act of faith possesses.

Or we could examine phenomenologically another state of affairs. I know Paul very superficially. I have met him and spoken to him on a few occasions. Still and all, the little that I know of him shows me clearly that he is a man of outstanding moral character. This intuition through which I form my image of Paul possesses a relatively low degree of certitude, much lower than the grade of certitude possessed by the intuition which I have of Peter. If nonetheless this intuition becomes the source of an act of faith, that act of faith will be endowed with a very high degree of certitude. The faith which I place in Paul possesses much more certitude than does the faith which I place in Peter—and this despite the fact that the intuition which I have of Peter has much more certitude than the intuition which I have of Paul.

The source of the degree of certitude in faith in a Thou is then the content of which the intuition is the medium, or rather, to put it even more accurately, it is the ontological perfection of the content, which in the case in point comes down to the ontological perfection or imperfection of an historical, concrete Thou. This is the intrinsic ground for the different degrees of certitude in the act of faith and in its object. Let us call this the "onto-logical" motive of faith. From this it becomes clear that there can be no question here of a logical motive.

The intuition which is the medium through which the "onto-logical" motive of faith becomes present to me can be called the intuition of trustworthiness. For we are always dealing here with a Thou endowed with a determined ontological perfection, and who, consequently, is also endowed with a determined degree of "trustworthiness." Trustworthiness is the personal ontological perfection of the Thou which becomes present to a human knower through the medium of the intuition.

The Personal Structure
of Supernatural Faith

1   The Problem

1. *The Biblical Concept of Faith.* The expression πίστις can signify in its profane use one's holding something as true. It can also mean trust, pledge, oath, covenant, fidelity and argument.[78] In the majority of cases πίστις means trust or fidelity.[79]

In the Old Testament, faith signifies the attitude of a person who recognizes Yahweh as God. In this attitude are included also trust, hope, fear and obedience. The "yes" spoken to Yahweh becomes, insofar as it is related to God's past actions, fidelity; and insofar as it is directed to the future, trust.[80]

It is understandable therefore that in the New Testament the concept of faith is endowed with a plenitude of meaning which makes it extremely difficult to analyze. The ex-

[78] De Broglie, *De Fide*, printed as a manuscript, Institut Catholique de Paris, 3–10.

[79] De Broglie, *De Fide*, 5.

[80] R. Bultmann, *Theologisches Wörterbuch zum Neuen Testament*, ed. G. Kittel and G. Friedrich, vol. 6, Stuttgart 1955, 198.

pression πίστις embraces so many possible meanings that the exegete is compelled to examine each passage in which it is used most carefully to see which one of the possible meanings should be attributed to it there. The exegetical problem, which underlines the effort to discover its proper meaning in each place where it is found, can be formulated somewhat as follows. What is the original meaning of πίστις and what concrete signification does it take on in this determined passage? By original meaning we mean here a general, or one might say a generic concept which, as the element to which the fundamental meaning of the term is attached, is given a more specific signification according to the concrete context in which it is used.

Is this "yes" spoken by the whole human person to Christ as the God-man the original meaning of πίστις? If we assume that it is, it will shed light on a good number of points connected with the act of faith. For the "yes" spoken to the teaching Christ is the condition of possibility for the "yes" which is said also to his statements. πίστις in this case would take on the determined meaning of a holding-to-be-true; in other words, taking-to-be-true would occupy the foreground of the term's plenitude of meaning. If I say "yes" to the commands of Christ, then πίστις takes on the idea of obedience. If I say "yes" to Christ when he promises salvation, then πίστις becomes trust. If I say "yes" to Christ who helped others through his miracles insofar as he can help me too, then πίστις takes on the meaning of belief in miracles.

Is such an interpretation of the essence of belief exegetically sound? Can it be said theologically that the original meaning of πίστις is the "yes" spoken by the whole human person to Christ the God-man?

2. *The Biblical and Dogmatic Concepts of Faith.* The words of the First Vatican Council would seem to militate against this interpretation of belief when it says: "*qua, Dei aspirante et adjuvante gratia, ab eo revelata vera esse credimus, . . . propter auctoritatem ipsius Dei revelantis.*"[81] Ought not we say therefore that the principal and original meaning of faith is holding something-to-be-true?

Such is not the case. The council has indeed laid down a truth of faith once and for all, and it has done so authoritatively and infallibly. The council did not however define that the words "*qua . . . ab eo revelata vera esse credimus*" were a logical definition of faith. The council wishes merely to emphasize the important and essential element of the act of faith, without implying that its words contain a logically complete definition which embraces all the essential elements of belief. In other words, the formulation of Vatican is to be understood in a positive but not in an exclusive sense.

The objection might be raised that, although the words of the Vatican Council are not to be taken as an exhaustive statement of the nature of the act of faith, they should certainly be taken as a definition in which faith is described in its specific structure. For the council wanted expressly to propose a positive doctrine on the act of faith. Not only was a false understanding of faith condemned, but, more than that, as often happened in the Vatican Council, a general and positive teaching was laid down. If then the

[81] Denz. 1789

act of faith is described by the Vatican Council, it is done to bring out clearly the specific nature of faith. Consequently, although the formulation of the council may not be a logical definition which embraces all the essential elements of faith, it is nonetheless a description of the specific structure of what the Church understands by faith. This must be accepted unconditionally. The council wanted to bring out clearly a specific characteristic of the act of faith in opposition to a heterodox understanding of it. But this does not mean that this specific characteristic excludes a generic, more general and consequently more central element. In brief, the fact that faith signifies essentially holding-statements-to-be-true does not imply that faith means only this, or that this is the principal and original meaning of faith.

What then is the original meaning of faith? What are the various specific characteristics which distinguish its different forms? Do these distinguishing characteristics necessarily belong to the essence of faith? Do they necessarily belong to the essence of belief insofar as it is justifying? How are they related to one another?

3. The *"Analysis Fidei."*   From the time of de Lugo until the present day the central problem in the theology of faith, the crux *theologorum,* has been the *analysis fidei.* This is the question of the relationship between certitude of faith and the *praeambula fidei;* or to put it in different words, the question of the source of the certitude of faith.

The act of belief is, to be sure, an *assensus firmus super omnia,* a certitude which is higher than any other. What then is the origin of this certitude? That it exists we know from the teaching of the Church and from tradition. But what is its source? On what does it rest? What kind of certitude is it? How can the act of faith, whose origin is the *praeambula fidei*, possess a much greater certitude than the *praeambula* possess themselves? Does the law of logic: *pejorem semper sequitur conclusio partem*, apply to the certitude of faith?

2   Attempts at a Solution

The number of theories that have been proposed up to the present concerning the essence of the act of faith is extremely large. Nonetheless, for purposes of orderly consideration, it is possible to divide the most important of them at least, as de Broglie has done, into five systems,[82] although obviously, in a rough division such as this, we shall not be able to consider the finer—and at times quite important—distinctions between the individual theories.

a)   First System—*Mystical Faith*.   The theory of faith proposed by the early scholastic theologians was characterized by its endeavor to reduce the certitude of faith to the light of grace with no consideration given to any other aspect of the problem. Spiritually, the early scholastics were still very close to the fathers, and like the fathers themselves they gave no consideration to the *praeambula fidei*. They knew one way of grounding the act of faith quite well. They could argue convincingly from miracles and prophecies. That line of argument however simply brings us back to *fides acquisita* (*fides suasa*). *Fides acquisita* however is

[82] De Broglie, *De Fide*, 175–190.

not the faith which justifies, it is simply a preliminary step
to the acquisition of faith in the proper sense. This *fides
acquisita*, the *praeambula fidei*, is a necessary condition for
faith. Yet we do not believe on account of them. We do not
believe because of miracles and prophecies, but *exclusively*
because of the inner light of grace. The light of grace alone
is the ground (*ratio*) of faith and of its certitude.

Thus, for example, Alexander of Hales writes:

[articles of faith] are the self-evident principles. For by these
very principles [faith] finds the reason why it believes them;
that is, the first Truth. Just as in other sciences we believe these
principles of themselves, so through grace we believe that God
is three and one . . . and the grace of faith is the reason through
which we argue to their truth.[83]

We can find similar statements in Duns Scotus.[84] Wil-
liam of Auvergne, in his theory on the act of faith, sees
faith in a somewhat different light. For him the act of faith
is an act of intellectual heroism, for we must accept in faith
the *veritates improbabiles*.[85]

The great deficiencies and dangers inherent in this theory
of faith are obvious today. Since the First Vatican Council
theologians can no longer speak as though a merely external

[83] III, q. 68, m. 6, a. 2 ad 3 contra 2 partem. Cited by de Broglie,
De Fide, 177.

[articuli fidei] sunt principia fidei per se nota. Cum ipsis enim
articulis [fides] invenit causam quare credat eis, scilicet primam
Veritatem. Sicut in aliis scientiis ipsa principia credimus propter
se, ita propter gratiam fidei credimus Deum esse trinum et unum
. . . et gratia fidei est qua arguitur eorum veritas.

[84] De Broglie, *De Fide*, 177.

[85] *Opera*, Paris 1674, *De Fide* c. 1, pp. 3–4; cited in de Broglie,
De Fide, 177.

and purely accidental relationship existed between the external signs of revelation and the act of faith. We know also that such a theory must lead to an extreme individualism in faith. For every Christian would have to appeal exclusively to his own inner experience of grace. We also know that the theory of "mystical belief" necessarily involves an inadmissible rigorism. For every error in matters of faith would indicate that there had been an inner disobedience to grace. There could be no such thing as a *peccatum mere materiale*; and every heretic would have to be a formal one.

b) SECOND SYSTEM—*Synthetic Belief.* Toward the middle of the thirteenth century the great scholastic theologians developed the synthetic theory of faith. Just as intellectual knowledge can arise only through the common action of the *phantasm* and the *intellectus agens*, so also can the act of faith come into being only through the common operation of the external signs of revelation and the inner light of faith. The purely sensible *phantasm* becomes under the light of the *intellectus agens* the *species intelligibilis*, and so also the *praeambula fidei* under the light of grace (*lumen fidei*) become faith, *fides*, itself.

The material object of the act of faith is therefore always a twofold one (which is believed however *per modum unius*): the individual religious truth and the fact that this truth was revealed. If then we believe in the Trinity, we also believe, *per modum unius*, that the mystery of the Trinity was revealed. Capreolus writes:

. . . by faith I assent first of all directly to this: "God has revealed that he is three and one," just as light is the primary object; and secondarily I assent to this: "God is three and one," as color is the secondary object; and this however is carried out in one and the same act.[86]

This is the *magnum fidei mysterium* of Suarez which has become so famous.[87]

The formal object, or perhaps, to put it better, the motive of the act of faith is the *auctoritas Dei revelantis*, insofar as it is visible in external revelation under the light of grace.[88] This theory of belief is attributed by de Broglie to Thomas of Aquinas, Richard of Middleton, Capreolus, Suarez, Bellarmine, Gregory of Valencia and in general to the older, non-Molinist Jesuits.[89]

The principal difficulty connected with the synthetic theory of belief in the opinion of many modern theologians is the *magnum mysterium* of Suarez. Can we say that every single truth is believed simultaneously and *natura simul* together with the supernatural character it possesses as a revealed truth? Why this *magnum mysterium*? What sense is there, we might object, in speaking of an *analysis fidei*, if, instead of explaining faith, we propose an explanation which comes down to the denial of the very possibility of its ex-

---

[86] In III Sent., d. 24, q. 1, a. 3, par. 4 ad 1; de Broglie, *De Fide*, 179.

. . . per fidem primo et directe assentio huic "Deus revelavit quod Deus est trinus et unus," sicut visus primo fertur in lucem; et secundario assentio huic, "Desu est trinus et unus," sicut visus secundario fertur in colorem; unico tamen et eodem actu.

[87] *De Fide*, dis. 3, s. 6, n. 8; cf. de Broglie, *De Fide*, 179.

[88] De Broglie, *Pour une théorie rationnelle de l'acte de foi*, vols. 1-2, Ad usum auditorum (printed as a manuscript), Institut Catholique de Paris.

[89] De Broglie, *De Fide*, 178.

planation? We assent in faith to the Trinity because God has revealed this mystery. Then the fact that God has revealed this mystery becomes the object of a second assent of faith. Thus faith is explained through faith. Can we, in all honesty, call this an explanation?

We might say in passing that the synthetic theory of faith, in the more developed form it has been given by modern theologians, is the most logical of all the existing theories. But since we will have to return to this subject once more in the course of our discussions, what has been said about it will be sufficient for the moment.

c) THIRD SYSTEM—*Syllogistic Faith.* The original author of the theory of faith which de Broglie calls "syllogistic faith" seems to have been Duns Scotus. Scotus proposed two theories of faith. One was the theory proposed by Alexander of Hales, the other was a new one. Scotus himself expressed no preference for one theory over the other. The second of the theories proposed by Scotus was taken up by the Nominalists, who made it their own. This is true particularly of Ockham and Gabriel Biel.[90]

In this theory of the *analysis fidei* it is taken for granted from the very beginning that grace has nothing to do with the intrinsic structure of the act of faith. The structure of the act of faith is always the same whether it is placed under the influence of grace or not. If an actual, historical act of faith should happen to be supernatural, that fact should be attributed to the will of God, since it could have been just as well a purely natural one. Consequently, any in-

[90] *Ibid.* 181–183.

quiry concerning the structure of the act of faith and its noetic relations must prescind completely from grace and the supernatural order as such. In no case and under no conditions can the certitude of the assent of faith be attributed to the light of grace. In this refusal to attribute the certitude of faith to the light of grace we see the sharp contrast between this theory and all the other attempts to solve the problem of the act of faith.

A second characteristic of this theory is the casual way in which it simply takes the historical fact of Christian revelation for granted. For it the fact of revelation presents no sort of a problem; it is simply taken as an admitted fact. This position, which is so difficult for us to understand, is doubtless due to the spirit of an age in which the historicity of revelation was accepted universally as self-evident. The collective consciousness of that age, singularly free, as it was, of heresy, holds firmly to the actuality of revelation without giving it a second thought. Only in this way can we understand how the theologians of the period could describe the intellectual assent to the fact of revelation as a non-free act, an *assensus necessarius*.[91]

Thus, for example, Gabriel Biel writes:

Just as I firmly believe without the slightest hesitation that the world preceded me and that parts of the world and cities exist which I have not seen . . . because I do not doubt the veracity of those who relate these truths . . . much less can I doubt the veracity of those preaching the faith, particularly in the light of the subsequent signs and miracles that have taken place. Consequently, I can firmly believe their preaching

[91] *Ibid.* 182.

through faith gained by means of their words and the witness of true signs.[92]

The act of faith can thus be reduced to a simple syllogism. The major premise consists of the truth: God cannot deceive us—*Deus est verax.* This truth is proposed as evident: *cuilibet naturaliter insita.*[93] The minor of the syllogism consists of the knowledge, possessed with certainty through an act of acquired faith (*fides acquisita*), that God has revealed this determined mystery. Thus can the act of faith be expressed in the following syllogism:

Si Deus aliquid revelat, illud verum est.

Atqui Deus Trinitatem revelavit.

Ergo Trinitas vera est.

Grace itself plays a subordinate role here. De Broglie writes in this connection:

Some, along with Scotus and Biel, say that the infused virtue of faith of itself first of all inclines the mind solely to the major premise "Whatever God says is true" and with the result that this major is held "more intensely" than it would be by the natural light of the mind. Thus once the minor (known through the merely natural light of the intellect) is accepted, the conclusion itself somehow participates in the supernaturality and the "intensity" of the major. Others along with Occam, (*Quol.* 3, q.7) think that faith inclines the mind not only toward the

[92] In III Sent., d. 23, p. 2, a. 1, concl. cited in de Broglie, *ibid.*

Sicut firmiter credo sine amni formidine de opposito mundum praecessisse me et partes mundi esse ac civitates quas non vidi . . . quia non dubito de veracitate narrantium . . . multo minus dubitare possum de veritate praedicantium fidem, maxime sequentibus miraculis et signis; et per consequens possum firmiter, fide per verbum eorum et signorum veracium testimonia acquisita, credere eorum praedicationi.

[93] Scotus, In III Sent., d. 23, no. 4.

major but also to the minor, which, therefore, itself is adhered to "more intensely" when infused faith is present. Thus we understand how the conclusion shares in the supernaturality and "intensity" of the premises from this twofold source.[94]

The difficulties inherent in this theory of faith are generally recognized. We might well ask ourselves whether the freedom and meritorious character of faith can be accounted for in a theory which reduces the act to a syllogism. If the major premise is a truth *cuilibet naturaliter insita*, and the minor is seen to be true as *sinc formidine de opposito*, then both premises are certain. Consequently, the conclusion possesses the same certitude as the premises. This would mean however that the act of faith is *cognitio certa* in and of itself, from which any element of freedom would have to be excluded. The freedom of faith would then involve nothing more than does our freedom to believe that Alexandria is really situated in North Africa. And we could ask as well in this case how it comes to pass that the assent of faith is an *assensus firmus super omnia*. For just as it must be applied to every syllogism, so the principle: *pejorem sequitur semper conclusio partem conclusio partem* would have to be applied

---

[94] De Broglie, *De Fide*, 182–183.

Alii, cum Scoto et Biel, dicunt virtutem infusam fidei primo et per se inclinare mentem in solam majorem "Quidquid Deus dicit est Verum," et afficere ut illa major "intensius" tenaetur quam in solo lumine naturali innotesceret. Hinc, accedente minore (per merum lumen naturale cognita), ipsa conclusio supernaturalitatem et "intensitatem" majoris quodammodo participat. Alii vero cum Occam (Quol. 3, q. 7) censent fidem inclinare non modo in majorem sed etiam in minorem, quae proinde, cum adest fides infusa, et ipsa "intensius" teneri censetur. Et sic etiam intelligitur quomodo duplici illo fonte conclusio supernaturalitatem et "intensionem" praemissarum participet.

as well to the syllogism of faith. Thus the assent of faith could possess no more certitude than the premises themselves. If however the assent of faith has no more certitude than its premises, then the assent of faith can be no longer called an *assensus firmus super omnia*.

d) FOURTH SYSTEM—*Fides Prudentialis.* This theory arose toward the end of the sixteenth century due to the influence of Molinism. According to the Molinist teaching, the content of a supernatural act of faith is no different from that of a corresponding natural act. The supernaturality of the act is confined in the Molinistic system exclusively to the subjectivity which is elevated by grace. Thus it can in no way change the content of the act, and consequently it cannot in any way become an object of consciousness. Therefore, as far as its conscious experienced content is concerned, the supernatural act of faith is in no way distinguished from an act of natural faith. And so in our endeavor to discern the structure of the act of faith, we can and indeed we must prescind from grace. There can be no light of grace as Thomas understood it.

This basic presupposition was accepted by both the Molinists and the Nominalists. Yet since they were well aware of the great difficulties intrinsic to the Nominalist theory of faith in its very primitive form, they felt obliged to approach their subject from a new point of view.

In opposition to the Nominalists, de Lugo insisted on the necessity of taking freedom into consideration in any inquiry into the structure of the act of faith. This freedom however, according to de Lugo, should not be looked for in the major premise: *quidquid Deus revelat est verum.* For this major is simply a conditional proposition which does not even presuppose the existence of God. The free element in the act of faith must therefore be found in the minor premise: *Deus hoc revelavit*.

De Lugo calls the major premise of the syllogism of faith a *judicium immediatum*. Its immediacy is not to be taken in the sense in which neo-scholastic epistemologists understand the term. This proposition is called immediate because it logically presupposes no human witnesses. The medium therefore which the term "immediate" excludes is the medium of a human witness. For we can see the truth of the proposition: *si Deus aliquid revelat, illud est verum* through a purely *a priori* intellectual reflection.

According to de Lugo the minor premise of the syllogism is also immediate; and in this we find the essence of his whole theory. Even here, says de Lugo, nothing comes to us through the medium of a human witness. Even the proposition: *Deus hoc revelavit*, is immediate. The fact of revelation is therefore, according to de Lugo, something which every man can and must know immediately, i.e. without the mediation of human faith. I can believe Peter if I speak with him. This is immediate knowledge (in de Lugo's sense of the term). Therefore I can believe Peter if he writes me a letter which Paul conveys to me. Even in this case my knowledge is immediate, for I do not believe Peter because I have first believed Paul, but because I read his letter which I recognize as his. So too in revelation, God reveals himself mediately, to be sure, that is, through the medium of sacred scripture, the preaching of his word, the testimony of the martyrs, etc. Yet immediately (without the intervention of

belief in a human person) I can know (i.e. believe) that
God is mediately revealing himself to me. Thus the minor
premise of the syllogism of faith is also immediate.

If however both the major and the minor premise of the
syllogism of faith are "immediate," then the conclusion is
"immediate" also. And since the act of faith is "immediate," it is not logically dependent on the faith I place in my
parents, teachers or anybody else. I do not believe in God
therefore because I believe my father and teacher when they
tell me that God revealed the Trinity. Admittedly, the
word of God comes to me mediately, that is, through the
medium of the Church, and finally through my father and
my teachers. But I know "immediately" that it is God himself who speaks to me through them. Because my faith is
"immediate," it is not logically dependent on the faith I
place in my father and my teachers. Thus I cannot say:
pejorem sequitur semper conclusio partem. My faith in
God therefore can possess much greater certitude than the
faith which I place in my parents and teachers. So it is that
faith can be an *assensus firmus super omnia.*

De Lugo endeavors to place the freedom of the act of
faith not in the major premise of the syllogism of faith, but
in the minor premise alone. He writes:

> We must examine the nature of human faith directed toward
> belief in the testimony of a man, asking, that is, whether we
> resolve it by invoking another motive, or remain satisfied with
> one. When, for example, I believe Peter's testimony concerning
> Paul's death, is the assent to Peter's testimony immediate or
> mediate because of another motive? And, of course, it cannot be
> denied that usually the assent is immediate and often evident,
> whereas at other times it is obscure and inevident. When I hear

his voice clearly which I know very well from past experience, the evidence for the assent to the fact that Peter is speaking seems to be physical. At other times it is less clear, so that if I hear Peter's voice from a distance or see his writing, I can have some qualms about whether it is really Peter's voice or writing. Nonetheless I may recognize such resemblance to Peter's voice and to his writing that, though it is not clearly evident, still I can judge with high probability that this is Peter's voice or writing. Likewise we may sometimes hear God's voice speaking to us clearly and evidently; in that case the assent to the fact that God is speaking would be immediate and evident. Usually however we hear not so clearly but obscurely, particularly when God speaks through his ministers and messengers. Then, though our judgement that it is God's voice or message or writing may be obscure and without evidence, nevertheless it can be an immediate assent . . . for a man is able without evidence to judge that this is the voice of God speaking mediately through his messenger. And this assent can be immediate and on it faith in revealed mystery may be based.[95]

[95] *De Fide,* Disp. 1, s. 7, no. 117. See de Broglie, *ibid.* 184.

Videndum est quomodo se habeat fides humana in ordine ad testimonium hominis credendum, an scilicet resolvamus illud in aliud motivum, an vero sistamus in illo. Quando v.g. credo Petro testanti Paulum obiisse, an tunc assensus quo judico Petrum id testari sit immediatus, an mediatus propter aliquod aliud motivum. Et quidem negari non potest plerumque esse assensum immediatum et saepe evidentem, aliquando obscurum et inevidentem. Quando enim audio ejus vocem clare, quam eliunde optime cognosco, videtur esse assensus evidens evidentia physica, quo judico Petrum loqui; aliquando vero est minus clarus, ut si audio vocem Petri distantis, vel video scripturam ipsius; possum enim in utroque casu formidare an vere sit vox scriptura Petri; video tamen tantam propositionem et similitudinem cum voce et scriptura Petri ut, licet non habeam claritatem et evidentiam, probabilissime tamen possem assentire quod haec sit vox vel scriptura Petri. Similiter ergo vox Dei loquentis posset aliquando clare et evidenter audire; et tunc assensus ille esset immediatus et evidens de locutione Dei. Plerumque tamen non ita clare auditur sed

Is then the act of faith itself a syllogism according to de Lugo? Or is it a single, nondiscursive act? It would appear to be the latter. For the expression "immediate" as de Lugo uses it seems to exclude not only the medium of human faith, but in addition every type of discursive thought. Consequently, the syllogistic structure of his theory of faith should be taken as simply the logical presentation of a process which in itself is really not discursive thought. As we understand it then the act of faith, according to de Lugo's theory, should be taken as a nondiscursive assent to a discursive content. In a genuine syllogism the major is assented to first (*natura et logice prius*), and then the minor and then the conclusion. However the syllogism of faith, as de Lugo presents it, is essentially different. The assent to the major, minor and conclusion are *natura et logice simul*.[96] The act of faith then, looked at as an intellectual operation, is not a syllogism. Whether, from the point of view of its content, it should be considered a syllogism can, as far as our discussion is concerned, be left an open question.

De Lugo's theory won many distinguished supporters. Among the greatest of them should be numbered Cardinal Franzelin, who not only displayed a masterly grasp of it, but

---

obscure, praesertim quando Deus loquitur per nuntios vel ministros, et tunc quidem, licet obscure et inevidenter, possumus tamen immediate credere illam esse vocem seu nuntium aut scripturam Dei . . . Potest enim homo inevidenter judicare hanc esse vocem Dei loquentis mediate per istum nuntium; qui assensus esse potest immediatus; et in ipso potest fundari fides mysterii revelati.

[96] De Broglie, *De Fide*, 185.

carried it further in developing its ecclesiological aspects. The Church and tradition are the medium through which we encounter the truth to be believed and the ground of our faith as well. We see not only the truth to be believed in, but also the miracles, prophecies and other signs, so that *obscure et inevidenter* but nonetheless "immediately" we can say our "yes" to the God who speaks to us "mediately."[97]

The weakness of this system lies above all in the fact that it cannot give a satisfactory explanation of how from a *praeambulum*, although it is still not evident, there can suddenly arise an *assensus firmus super omnia*. For according to de Lugo, the reality of revelation is known as such only *obscure et inevidenter*. Should a man consider it prudent nonetheless (*probabilissime tamen possim assentire . . .*) to assent to it, his assent may be naturally very prudent but it is not yet on that account alone an *assensus firmus super omnia*. And if it is nonetheless an *assensus firmus super omnia*, then it can well be asked what is the source of this increase in certitude, for it is not contained in the *praeambula*. What is the source of this certitude insofar as it exceeds the measure of the *probabilissime possim assentire?* If de Lugo says that it comes from grace, then he has abandoned his fundamental presupposition that grace in no way can become an object of consciousness or exert a causal influence on it, and he has returned to the position of Thomas and the older scholastics. If however he says that an increase in certitude should be ascribed to the influence of free will,

[97] J. B. Franzelin, *Tractatus de divina traditione et scriptura*, Rome 1875, 2nd ed.

then it might well be asked how the will as such can be the ground of a rational certitude. And if he were to maintain that nonetheless it is, then the question could well be raised whether this certitude can any longer be considered *rationalis*. Another objection which can be raised against de Lugo's theory is that the relationship between the act of faith and the *auctoritas Dei revelantis* is given too little consideration. The act of faith for de Lugo seems to rely more on man's own intelligence than on the *auctoritas Dei revelantis*.[98] And so faith seems to lose the character of a theological virtue.

e) FIFTH SYSTEM—*Fides Obsequiosa*. According to de Broglie the first outlines of this system can be found in the works of a number of seventeenth century theologians, particularly Elizalde and Thyrsus Gonzales.[99] It was then adopted toward the end of the nineteenth century by a good number of theologians, among them Schiffini, Billot, Bainvel and van Noort.[100]

The basic presupposition of this theory is that we must solve the noetic problem of the act of faith without appealing to the light of grace. In this they stand together with de Lugo against the older theologians. In opposition to de Lugo however they intend to explain its increase in certitude, an element which, as we recall, was left completely unexplained in de Lugo's system. Moreover they wish to defend the character of faith as a genuinely theological virtue.

[98] De Broglie, *De Fide*, 186.
[99] *Ibid.* 186–187.
[100] Harent, *DTC* VI, 55–514.

The fundamental principle of this theory can be explained in the following way. Preliminary to the act of faith we must have certitude in relation to the veracity of God and also to the fact of revelation. Before we can place the act of faith then we must know with certainty that God is truthful and that he has revealed this definite truth. The two propositions therefore which according to de Lugo were the major and minor premises of the syllogism of faith and were assented to simultaneously *logice simul* with the conclusion become in the *fides obsequiosa* system the presuppositions of faith. In other words, propositions which for de Lugo were part of the logical contents of the act of faith become in this theory no longer part of the content of the act of faith, but rather its presuppositions.

Different theologians give different explanations as to how we attain certitude concerning the veracity of God and the fact of revelation. They differ also in their endeavor to determine the nature of this certitude more exactly. Some consider it a certitude whose ground is *evidentia proprie dicta*, while for others it is a certitude whose ground is *evidentia imperfecta* (*evidentia relativa*)—a certitude equivalent to the *assensus prudentialis* of de Lugo.[101]

The veracity of God and the fact of revelation must be known prior to the act of faith, since only the individual revealed truths and not the fact of revelation are the object of the act of faith. As in human faith so also in *fides divina*, what is said is the object of belief, not the fact that it was said.

If however both the veracity of God and the fact of revela-

[101] De Broglie, *De Fide*, 187.

tion are certainly believed prior to the act of faith, then the individual truths proposed for our belief must also be known and assented to prior to the act of faith. For if I assent to the proposition: *Quidquid Deus dicit est verum;* if in addition I assent to the proposition: *Deus dicit se esse trinum,* then I also assent to the logical conclusion of these premises: *Deus est trinus.* Assenting to the veracity of God and to the fact of revelation means then assenting to the individual revealed truths. This assent to the individual revealed truths however is not the act of faith itself. It too is but a mere presupposition required for faith. It possesses no more certitude than the two premises. The problem of the act of faith is really to show how from this "pre-belief" (as we may call it) the act of faith in the proper sense arises. Opinions vary widely on this point. De Broglie gives a masterly summary of the various opinions.

But to explain how that free assent made in homage (or obedience) to God can be distinguished from the preliminary assent to a truth revealed by God is arrived at as the conclusion to a syllogism, the aforementioned authors go through quite a few contortions. The first condition for the assent of faith and the possibility of its being freely super-added to syllogistic knowledge (to the preamble itself as conceived) is that this assent be able to be distinguished and actually be distinguished, by reason of its object, from the assent to the *praeambula.* What is more, it does not readily appear in just what this distinction can consist. For not only is the same material object affirmed in both assents, but there seems to be no distinction either in the formal object or the motive, since in either case the motive for assent seems to be the same supreme veracity of the divine witness. . . .

To free themselves from this difficulty, the defenders of this system branch off in three main directions:

1. Some[102] introduce at this point the amazing distinction between the double truth affirmed in the material object; as if, so to speak, it were one thing to know the truth of something spoken as such and another thing to know the truth of the thing expressed by speaking. Thus they conclude that the divine veracity suffices to demonstrate syllogistically the truth of the proposition "God is Three Persons," but that in the process the ability to believe or disbelieve that the divine reality is in itself threefold, is left intact. . . .

2. Others offer at this point the subtle distinction between a twofold mode of believing on the authority of God, by distinguishing between the assent which is given because of the previous knowledge of the authority of God from the assent which is given because of the very authority of God known previously. . . .

3. Then however there are these (above mentioned) authors who seek refuge in another's distinction: between the twofold authority of God on account of which the truth of what is revealed can be believed. Billot distinguishes between an assent "which rests on the evidence of true testimony (as when the historian believes what is narrated in concordant contemporary testimony)" and the assent which rests on the witness' authority formally as authority (as is the case when a boy believes his mother, or the scholar his master, or as in those things which pertain to ordinary daily intercourse, everyone believes what he hears from an honest man solely because, as may be presumed, he is worthy of belief!). [103] He thinks that the assent given in the first case "is given purely and simply because it is evident to the intellect that in testifying, the one giving testimony can neither deceive nor be deceived"; in the second case assent is given not precisely and formally because of the conspicuous evidence of the true testimony, but because the dignity of the one giving testimony makes him trustworthy . . . and this manner of believing is significantly different from the preceding . . . because the knowledge and veracity of the witness, which can suffice for the faith mentioned in the first case, is not sufficient for the

[102] Harent, *DTC* VI, 418, 421.
[103] L. Billot, *De Ecclesia*, Rome 1898, 41.

faith with which we are now concerned. For that there be evidence in the witness it suffices that we see that the witness in a given instance was not in fact in error and in fact did not lie . . . But in the present case the motive of assent is the dignity of the speaker or his right to the submission of our mind . . . which dignity indeed . . . is in him alone who . . . is gifted with knowledge and veracity![104] This distinction indeed . . .[105]

[104] *Ibid.* 39–40.
[105] De Broglie, *De Fide*, 188–189.

Sed ad explicandum quomodo distingui possit ille assensus liber sic in obsequium Dei exercitus ab ipso assensu praeambulo in veritatem a Deo revelatum, qui per modum conclusionis syllogisticae obtinetur, mirum in modum auctores praedicti insudant. Prima enim condicio ut assensus ille libere superaddi possit cognitioni syllogisticae (ipsi, ut fingitur, praeambulae) est ut scl. assensus ille distingui possit et distinguatur, ex parte sui objecti, ab ipso illo assensu praembulo. Jam vero non facile apparet in quonam illa distinctio consistere possit. Non modo enim in utroque assensu idem objectum materiale affirmatur, sed ne ex parte quidem objecti formalis seu motivi videtur esse diversitas, cum in utroque casu motivum assentiendi videatur esse eadem summa veracitasdivini testis . . .

A qua difficultate ut se expediant, defensores systematis in tres vias abeunt:

I. Nonnulli miram hic distinctionem introducunt inter duplicem veritatem objecti materialiter affirmandi: quasi scl. aliud esset cognoscere veritatem alicujus dicti qua talis, aliud vero cognoscere veritatem ipsius rei per dictum expressae. Unde concludunt veracitatem divinam sufficere quidem ad syllogistice demonstrandam veritatem enuntiationis "Deus est trinus in personis," per hoc tamen integram relinqui facultatem credendi vel discredendi quod ipsa realitas divina secundum se trina sit . . .

II. Alii subtilem hic afferunt distinctionem inter duplicem modum credendi propter Dei autoritatem, distinguendo scl. assensum qui datur propter ipsam cognitionem praeviam auctoritatis Dei ab assensu qui datur propter ipsam auctoritatem Dei praevie cognitam . . .

III. Inde tandem auctores praedicti in aliam distinctionem

We can already see the principal difficulty with this theory from de Broglie's summary. It lies in the difference between the act of faith in the proper sense and the assent to the revealed truths given prior to the act of faith. The various attempts at a solution to the problem also show very clearly that it is here that its real problem confronts this system. For the theologian who faces facts can never make a distinction between assent to a proposition (*enuntiabile*) and the assent to the fact (*res*) expressed in the proposition. Neither can we understand how in such a case any objective, realistic meaning can be given to the *praeambula fidei*.

confugiunt: inter duplicem Dei auctoritatem, propter quam veritati revelatorum credi possit. Distinguit enim Billot assensum "qui nititur evidentia veri testimonii (sicut cum historicus credit ea quae in consentientibus testimoniis coaevis narrata reperit)" et assensum "qui nititur attestantis auctoritati formaliter sub ratione auctoritatis (sicut cum puer credit matri, et indoctus docto, vel cum in iis quae ad ordinarium vitae commercium pertinent, unusquique credit audita a viro honesto, unice quia ut praesumere licet, dignus est ille cui fidatur)." Et censet in priore casu assensum dari "pure et simpliciter quia evidens intellectui est quod in testificando testificans nec falli potuit nec fallere"; in altero vero assensum dari "non praecise et formaliter propter affulgentem evidentiam veri testimonii, sed propter dignitatem quam habet testificans ut fidatur sibi . . . Et hic modus multum differt a praecedenti . . . quia scientia et veracitas testis quae sufficere potest ad fidem priore modo dictam, non sufficit ad fidem de qua in praesenti. Etenim ad hoc ut habeatur evidentia in attestante, satis est ut appareat testem in casu determinato non fuisse de facto in errore et de facto non esse mentitum . . . At vero in praesenti motivum assensus est dignitas vel jus loquentis ad docilem mentis acquiescentiam . . . quae quidem dignitas . . . est in eo solo qui . . . instruitur habitu scientiae et veracitatis." Haec sane distinctio . . .

We must also insist, in opposition to the distinction between *cognitio auctoritatis Dei* and *auctoritas Dei cognita*, that a distinction such as this can have no place in a realistic system. For the *cognitio auctoritatis Dei* is only the motive of the act of faith insofar as it is the medium through which God's authority as such is known. *Cognitio* as such is not the motive for an assent; but the motive is rather what is known in it, the *auctoritas Dei*. And if, in spite of this, one wants to hold the opposite opinion, then, if he is to be consistent, he will have to maintain that the *cognitio* as such, and consequently every *cognitio*, can be the motive of an act of faith; and then it can be so equally well, no matter what is known in the *cognitio*, be it large or small, good or bad, endowed with the authority or utterly devoid of it. We would have to say then that even lack of authority could be the motive of an act of faith. But this is an open contradiction.

Even Billot's final attempt at a solution hardly seems to be sufficient. For the *dignitas loquentis* is contained both in the act of faith and in the knowledge prior to faith. It is found in both cases. The *dignitas loquentis* in God is his nature insofar as it is considered under this aspect. But this nature is assented to and known both in prior knowledge and in the act of faith itself. How can it be then that in the one case, that of the act of faith, it should be the motive sufficient for an assent, while in the other case, that of our knowledge prior to faith, it should not be?

Our outline of the five main systems of the *analysis fidei* has been, as we emphasized at its beginning, rather primitive and sketchy. The different theories had to be simplified for purposes of summary description. Our chief concern however has not been to follow out the line of thought of the diverse individual theologians. We were interested simply in providing a brief survey of the different tendencies in the scholastic theology of the act of faith; and in an exposition of this kind it is not the details which matter, but rather the fundamental concepts of the different systems.

Yet even this brief summary shows that much is left undecided in this theology. Scholastic theologians are much concerned with a single problem. They wish to explain without contradicting themselves both the freedom and the certitude of the act of faith. To do so they must explain the relation between the act of faith and the *praeambula*, and the relation between grace and free will. There are differences of opinion about practically all these areas, and the important points concerning which there is in fact a *consensus theologorum* are very few in number. If we turn our attention to modern theologians, the picture is essentially the same. Aubert's remarkable monograph[106] on the act of faith has given a good summary of the different attempts at a solution.

3   The Personal Structure of "Fides Divina"

1. *Summary and Synthesis.*   Let us now attempt to outline the main elements in the metaphysical structure of *fides divina*. We begin with the presupposition that God has revealed himself through Christ and that the act of faith, as

[106] R. Aubert, Le problème de l'acta de foi. Donnés traditionnelles et resultats des controverses récents, Louvain 1950, 2nd ed.

a fundamental act in the order of salvation, possesses a supernatural character. We shall then apply the results of our metaphysical inquiry into the *a priori* of faith to *fides divina*, on the supposition that *fides divina* cannot be totally different from interpersonal faith. Using this as a basic presupposition we can then describe the evolution of *fides divina* in the following way.

I know on the basis of pre-scientific reflection that there exists one being, who transcends the finite universe, and that this being is a personal God. This God, who is the Absolute Person, rules and directs the world. I know that this God is a person and that therefore he can enter into personal communication with me. This possibility of a personal communication on the part of God, this possibility of a divine revelation, must be kept always before my eyes. It is possible that my God may speak to me some day; it is possible that he has already spoken.

Then one day I encounter Christ. This encounter for us is always mediate. This means that I become acquainted with him through another person. It may be that I read the gospels. And so I form for myself gradually an image of Christ. I see him in the midst of his disciples, in conflict with the Pharisees. I hear his words when he talks to the sinful woman, when I see how he heals the sick, how he restores Lazarus to life. I follow him along the way of his passion; and see him in agony, I see him nailed to the cross. Then I hear that Mary and Peter have seen the Risen Lord. He is risen from the dead. He shows himself to the twelve and to many others; and then he sends them out into the whole world, *docentes et baptizantes*.

I read how the disciples, conscious of their mission, go into every country, and proclaim the message of joy; and how in their deaths they manifest Christ. I see how the first Christians form a community; how this community acquires its structure in accordance with the natural law and the positive command of Christ. I follow the history of this community, this Church throughout the long centuries. Before the eye of my mind its long history passes in review, a history of persecution, martyrdom, Christian emperors, saints, bishops and monks. I hear of good and bad popes, of good and evil times. I perceive that there is in the Church both injustice and a lack of holiness. Yet I see also that the Church, in spite of all this, continues to hold fast to Christ's doctrine, and that always—indeed, especially in her darkest hours— she is the mother of a glorious array of saints.

At first this is simply a conglomeration of many acts of knowledge. In some of its aspects it is highly developed and rich in content, while in respect to others it is confined to a few fundamental characteristics. It may be now that I begin to reflect upon my knowledge discursively. I ponder over the historicity of the gospels, the veracity of the contemporary witnesses, the authenticity of tradition. But gradually this totality of my knowledge begins to take on a form and shape. The individual acts of knowledge relate themselves to a single, large intuition. And in this single intuition I see the one, single, holy God who speaks to me through Christ and through his Church. Every single element of knowledge is formed into the totality present in this one great intuition. At this moment something new occurs. If perhaps up to this point I was still hesitant; if I still possessed no certitude by reason of my conceptual-discursive thought; if I did not know whether, after all, this was just an illusion, now all my uncertainty falls away. I know for sure that God speaks to me in Christ. This intuitive certitude (which we can develop in a conceptual-discursive manner, that is, scientifically) is given to me all at once.

If we try to account for this certitude in a reflective but still pre-scientific manner, we would say then to ourselves: in this man Christ I find the acme of all possible human perfection. He is simply incomparable. Now the fundamental, all-embracing idea possessed by Christ is his consciousness of mission: the Father, who is God, has sent me. If this belief is false, and yet constitutes Christ's spiritual inner center in which all that he said and did has its origin and source, then Christ is either a fool or a deceiver, or else he is what he claimed to be: the Son of God. But he cannot be a deceiver or a fool, for my picture of Christ is simply incompatible with deception or lunacy. Therefore he is the Son of God, in whom we find God's revelation of himself.

This intuition, which conveys to me, as it were, in an ordered series of levels, the Church, the man Christ and the word of God, possesses a compelling character. On the basis of this intuition I know (with some degree of certitude) that God has revealed himself and that I ought to respond to the word of God with total obedience. The degree of certitude in this intuition can vary very much. Nevertheless some degree of certitude must be present, otherwise no genuine intuition could be possessed as a medium through which we touch reality.

What we described above corresponds to what is called

in scholastic terminology the *judicium credibilitatis* and *judicium credenditatis*. Our interpretation coincides for the most part with what is common theological teaching today. The *praeambula fidei* must be known with certitude; and they must be known prior to the act of faith. The physical and moral miracles testify to the divine character of revelation. Then arise the *judicium credibilitatis* and *judicium credenditatis*. We differ from the common view however in that we maintain that this important process does not take place merely in judgments and concepts. Certainly concepts and judgments play a role in this process, but the primary factor is the intuition. This view is not only in accord with our theory on intuition; it also corresponds immediately with the phenomena. Indeed, it is the only view which corresponds with the phenomena. For the form of knowledge which is sufficient to justify the act of faith has been described by all who were converted as adults (and who were therefore able to give an account of the genesis of faith) as being not a discursive form of knowledge, but rather an intuitive one. It may be said in addition that, in most cases, this intuition of credibility is not experienced as such, because the act of faith in the proper sense arises from it with temporal immediacy, so that a grasp of the distinction through a phenomenological reflection on experience is scarcely possible.

This intuition contains not only an abstract credibility and the abstract *credenditas* corresponding to it, but more than that, an image of Christ and the Church around which all the content of revelation centers itself organically. They are the ex-pression of Christ. Although this concrete whole has, of course, as a whole, the character of *credibilitas* and *credenditas*, that which primarily possesses this character is whatever in it is revelation or pertains immediately to revelation: Christ in his historical concreteness.

This intuition now becomes an act of faith. Because it contains something personal, and because it is directed to the personal element in man, it demands a personal attitude, a decision coming from the total personality the personal content of which it is the medium. If man now makes a free decision, if he takes a positive stand toward Christ, this intuition becomes the cognitive element of this attitude. The intuition itself is one of the constituents of this attitude; and, as we know, the cognitive moment of the free attitude of personal knowledge is a personal act of faith.

Thus, since I utter my personal "yes" to Christ in his concrete historical fullness, I say "yes" to everything belonging to that fullness. And so I assent to his assertions; I accept them as true. *Fides divina* is therefore my personal "yes" spoken to the person of Christ and to the God who reveals himself in him. It is a personal "yes" spoken to his teaching. Or to put it briefly, it is a personal "yes" spoken to Christ, who is present—who speaks and acts.

We know from the sources of revelation that this *actus fidei* springs from the grace of God. Christ himself is grace; his words, and his teaching are graces—objective graces. All knowledge of this objective grace can arise only through the light of subjective grace. This inner *a priori* corresponds to the external object. Grace therefore has a role to play in everything; it exists everywhere. Not only are the *praeambula* known through the light of grace, but the decision to believe is also taken through the light of grace.

2. *The Object of Faith.*   We know from our metaphysical reflection that the object of faith is twofold; the personal Thou and the assertions grouped about this Thou, which belong to the historical concreteness of this Thou. In other words, the objects of faith are the Thou and his assertions. Corresponding to these two levels of the object of faith are, as we have distinguished, two types of faith itself: faith in a Thou and faith in an assertion. This distinction should also be applied to *fides divina.*

The faith in a Thou in *fides divina* is, according to our presuppositions, nothing other than the divine Thou itself revealed in Christ and his Church. To put it more precisely, it is the personal Thou of Christ, who exists as a Person in both his divine and human natures, who is the direct and immediate object of supernatural faith. Since however the personal Thou of Christ, his Person, is essentially trinitarian (which means that it can only be understood as a relation), the personal Thou of the Father and of the Holy Spirit are given with it as they exist together in the Trinity. Whoever then says "yes" to the Thou of Christ says "yes" also to the Father in the Holy Spirit.

It is evident that Christ's human as well as his divine nature, the Church and many other elements unite to constitute the total object of this faith in a Thou. For the believer says "yes" to Christ in his fullness and not to any kind of abstract universal.

Faith-in-an-assertion in *fides divina* consists of all the assertions which as peripheral elements of the Thou are included in the "yes" spoken to it in faith-in-a-Thou. Such statements are all *veritates fide divina credendae;* and this means all truths which God has revealed to men. We could go further here and work out an ordering of these truths. We could speak of an *objectum primarium* and *secundarium* in faith-in-an-assertion. We will content ourselves however with referring our reader to what has been already written on this subject in the various treatises on the act of faith.[107]

If we compare the results of our reflections with the data of theological tradition, then we discover that what we have deduced from our theory concerning the object of faith is in complete accord with what has been said about it by the magisterium of the Church and by tradition. The professions of the Christian faith found in the various credos give sufficient testimony to the fact that the central element in the object of faith is the three divine persons who reveal themselves in Christ. In like manner, the teaching and actions of Christ are considered to belong to the object of faith.[108] The only real differences therefore between the traditional interpretation and our theory of faith are found in the distinction which we have introduced between faith in a Thou and faith in an assertion, and in the fact that we have laid greater stress than theologians have been accustomed to do up to the present on the point that the personal Thou is the central element of the object of faith.

3. *The Certitude of Faith.* In our theory on the nature of the act of faith the certitude of faith does not arise from the certitude of the intuition (ontogenetic aspect), but

[107] De Broglie, *De Fide:* H. Lennerz, *Virtutibus Theologicis,* Rome 1933, 3rd ed.

[108] H. Vignon, *De Virtutibus et Donis Vitae Supernaturalis,* vol. I, Rome 1947/1948, 180–200.

rather from the content of faith itself. In other words, the firmitas of the act of faith is not proportioned to the firmitas of the intuition of credibility, but rather to the ontic-moral reality of the personal Thou to whom, as the content of our act of faith, our "yes" is spoken.

We have seen that we possess an extremely certain intuition of Peter, and that, nevertheless, our faith in him has a very limited firmitas. The reason for this is that the content of this intuition shows me that Peter is a truly wretched individual. Paul, on the contrary, is scarcely known to me. I possess an intuition of him whose formal certitude is very limited. Nonetheless the little that I know of him makes it clear to me that he is an excellent, most trustworthy man. Thus I put much more faith in Paul than I do in Peter. In other words, it is not the formal certitude of the intuition of credibility but rather its content, i.e. the ontological value of the Thou, which is the measure of the certitude of faith.

If we apply this principle to fides divina, it follows that the certitude of fides divina can be deduced in no way whatsoever from the certitude of the praeambula of the intuition of credibility. The degree of certitude possessed by the praeambula is a matter of little or no importance, provided that some kind of genuine certitude is found in them. The certitude of the intuition of credibility differs with every man. Since however the certitude of faith cannot, by any means, be deduced from the certitude of the praeambula, it is simply impossible to apply here the principle: pejorem sequitur semper conclusio partem. If we try to apply this principle here, then we are implicitly presupposing something which has not been proven, viz. that the certitude of faith must be proportioned to the certitude of the intuition of credibility.

We showed above that the certitude of faith (in its degrees) can be deduced from the personal perfection, from the ontic-moral value of the Thou, to whom our "yes" is spoken in "faith." The degree of certitude corresponds to the personal ontological value of the Thou. Since now however the Thou of *fides divina* possesses the highest possible ontic-moral perfection, the certitude of *fides divina* must be greater and more perfect than that of every other certitude: *assensus firmus super omnia*. For only a certitude of the highest type could correspond to the ontological value of the Thou to whom our "yes" is spoken in faith, since in this "Thou" we find the greatest ontological perfection possible.

The fact that the degree of certitude of belief corresponds always and necessarily to the degree of perfection possessed by the Thou does not mean that this certitude is not free. On the contrary, this certitude is only possible in faith and therefore only in the free personal attitude of the total human personality. Man can always say "no," and thus place a positive act of nonbelief. If his attitude however is a positive one, then this will be in accord with the reality to which its "yes" is spoken; and this means that its degree of certitude will correspond to the degree of perfection possessed by the Thou.

We have already tried at considerable length to establish that the certitude of faith is always greater and more perfect than the certitude of the intuition of credibility prior to belief. The act of faith, be it natural or supernatural, is always more perfect and more certain than the intuition prior to it. Between intuition and the act of faith there lies an *a priori* of personal knowledge which produces from the intuition the more perfect act of faith.

Logically, therefore, the certitude of *fides divina* is completely independent. The act of faith is its own logical motive; it is logical self-motivation. Should the question arise concerning the *ratio propter quam datur assensus*, that question is no longer concerned with a logical motive. We defined the logical motive as knowledge of something on which another knowledge of something else is logically dependent. If nonetheless we wish to designate a *ratio propter quam datur assensus*, then we will have to point to the ontic-moral value of the personal Thou, which, in that case, could be called the ontological or transcendental motive.

If we compare what we have deduced concerning the certitude of *fides divina* with the positive data of the magisterium of the Church and of tradition, then a necessary consequence of our theory is the *firmitas super omnia* of which they speak.

4. *The Freedom of Faith.* Every act of faith is always and necessarily the cognitive element of a personal free attitude toward a Thou. We cannot conceive of faith without freedom. Still further, freedom constitutes faith, for the cognitive and volitional moments of the free decision mutually constitute each other. From this it follows that even *fides divina* is an act of free knowledge. This freedom is not any kind of freedom whatsoever, not simply a *liberum in causa*. The act of faith itself can only be understood as a partial element of a concrete act of freedom and it is there-

fore free in an eminent sense. On this point too the result of our deduction is in perfect accord with tradition.[109]

5. *The "Praeambula Fidei."* Every act of faith, even *fides divina*, presupposes an intuition of credibility from which it arises. This intuition of credibility must be endowed with genuine certitude. It is prior to faith which has in it its ontological origin.

The intuition of credibility therefore is prior even to *fides divina*. This intuition, these *praeambula fidei*, must be possessed of genuine certitude. In this intuition faith in the proper sense has its origin. Here too the results of our reflection coincide with the venerable teaching of tradition.[110]

6. *The Light of Faith.* In every act of faith there must be, with respect to the intuition prior to it, an increase in knowledge, and consequently also an increase in certitude. This we have called "the natural light of faith." Thus there is also an increase in knowledge and certitude in *fides divina*; and so, in *fides divina* too there is a "natural light of faith."

Beyond this however we find in *fides divina* a supernatural light of faith. We have taken it for granted that *fides divina*, as the basic act in the supernatural order of salvation, is itself supernatural. This means however that the *a priori* of faith, which is a natural *a priori* in itself, has been supernaturally elevated. The act of faith therefore is itself supernatural and, consequently, endowed with even greater ontological perfection. Because it is higher in the realm of being, it must entail an increase in knowledge and certitude. Since however this increase is consequently purely supernatural,

---

[109] De Broglie, *De Fide*, 231–234.
[110] *Ibid.* 241–262.

we can speak of a supernatural light of faith. Or, to put it in concrete terms, without grace we would believe in God as a servant believes his master. Since however we are in the order of grace, our faith is that of children toward their father. This faith implies a growth in perfection, an increase in knowledge and certitude. In other words, corresponding to the elevation of the personal nature of the act of knowledge, there goes an elevation of the "quality of its knowledge" and of its certitude.[111]

7. *The Proposition of Faith.* Every act of faith is an act of intuitive knowledge, and thus the act of *fides divina* must be intuitive in its nature also. In other words, in *fides divina*, the universal is known in the concrete singular without any separation of subject and predicate and without discourse or the use of concepts.

Nevertheless, just as we analyze the intuition and from it form concepts and judgments, so too we analyze interpersonal belief. This manner of proceeding must be applied to *fides divina*, and thus from it as well concepts are abstracted and judgments formed. Even here the general principle is still true that the concepts and judgments derived from intuitive knowledge are always simply an aspect of the whole, and thus are always in need of further development.

If we analyze *fides divina*, the result will be the faith-proposition. This is an endeavor to express through the medium of conceptual and discursive thought the content of the intuitive *fides divina*.

[111] We cannot overemphasize the fact that what we are dealing with here is in no way quantitative. The increase in question therefore is not quantitative but a qualitative one.

If this analysis of *fides divina* is carried out on the level of scientific reflection, then a theological system comes into being. A theological system therefore is a conscious analysis carried out with toil and effort. As a consequence, every theological system is subject to the laws of history and remains in principle always open to further development. This implies that it will never be free from the necessity for improvement and further development. It is here that we find the metaphysical ground of possibility for the so-called "development of dogma."